YES,
I AM GENERALISING

A Bird's Eye View of The Black Society

By Tebogo Kenneth Monoametsi

DEDICATION

I dedicate this book to my parents who never had a chance to study yet still managed to raise kids they can be proud of.

To my dear mother in Heaven, you passed away suddenly before witnessing the full greatness of your kids unfold. May your dear soul rest in peace. Heaven is blessed, and I hope they managed to make you rest because you were always busy like your name Mmatiro.

To my mother-in-law, thank you for being a wonderful mother in all the years I have been welcomed into the family. I have never once felt that I'm an outsider. Thank you for your continuous support.

To my dad, you are still my hero. You did a good job. Thank you for raising a boy child to be an all-round responsible man, against all odds.

ACKNOWLEDGMENTS

I give all the praise to God for the inspiration and years of listening to all my prayers without prejudice.

I thank my wife for always believing in me and supporting me through thick and thin with all my factory faults. I don't know how you do it but thank you very much.

To my brothers and sisters, thank you for always supporting me and my family.

To my sons, I hope one day you will grow up to be respectable men of honour and reach for the sky always.

Lastly, I would like to thank all my friends who supported me through this journey; my constant demands for feedback and tapping your brains. God bless you all.

TABLE OF CONTENTS

FOREWORD

In his racy and humorous book, my friend Tebogo (who I prefer to call Tebza), has shone a light on everyday life in a typical Black township in the 80s. Tebza has chronicled his experience of life in Soweto during his formative years. However, his experiences resonate with anyone who grew up in any township during this period, irrespective of their geography within the four provinces of the country as was the case then.

Even though I pre-date Tebza by almost a decade and grew up in a tiny township on the outskirts of Durban called Clermont, I can identify with most of the antics that Tebza has reminisced about in this book. These take you back to a time where life was so simple and carefree where fun, play, and companionship were our everyday experience. A time when the adults had to carry the burden of eking out a living under very difficult circumstances. A time when words like 'overdraft' 'bond', 'stress' were foreign to us.

Tebogo has ultimately challenged us to draw from the values that were inculcated in us during the formative years described above, to propel ourselves to being exemplary citizens who live purposeful lives driven by a clear vision of making ours the best and thriving society. By drawing from our common experience, we can rekindle the hope and drive that propels us through the difficult 80s and strive towards claiming our just and rightful share of the fruits of our freedom and democratic order.

Thank you, my friend, for using your talent to take the reader on this wonderful journey. I invite everyone to enjoy the ride...

Eugene Zungu

1

INTRODUCTION

The concepts and ideas in this writing are purely opinion-based and not research-based. They comprise observations and personal experiences including reading of materials and articles. The objective is to bring forth awareness and discussions that can be well-researched and challenged. There is no one size fits all. Everyone can use their own discretion on facts over opinion and anything can be freely challenged. I chose a platform I understand better, which is writing my opinions down.

The intention is to cover observations of being born black and raised in a township, all the behavioural patterns, ideas, education, money, crime, lifestyle and other aspects.

I was born in Soweto, Meadowlands, Zone 1, famously called *Ndofaya* (I don't know how that name came about but I know one musician made it famous. The musician by the name of Kamazu, in his song, he says, "*Endofaya kusuka amaphepha, kusala amakhatbox*," loosely translated that 'only the weak leave' *Ndofaya*, but hardcore people remain). Meadowlands is famous for having different zones, from Zone 1 to Zone 11 — Meadowlands Hostel (those in my age group will know).

What makes Zone 1 special is the language most of my peers inherited from our elders called *Selesta*. That language is a way to communicate and confuse everyone else around who doesn't understand it. It takes words from the back and puts them in front. Sounds easy but in a conversation with the masters of the language, one is left dumbfounded and puzzled. (examples of *Selesta*; *motho* (human) would be pronounced *thomo*. In a sentence like, *motho o tshwere thipa* (A person with a knife), it would sound like, *thomo o retshwe pathi*. Most people from zones 2, 3, 7, 8 and 9 would follow as they had Tswana and Sotho heritages. The Zulu, Venda and Tsonga would struggle a bit until they had friends who spoke *Selesta*.

I'm a late 70s child, and now in my early 40s as I write this, therefore I will be biased towards certain age groups as this might be true to my age peers, including those born in the 80s and possibly the 90s. The 2000s as they are famously called have a totally different mindset which most of us are parenting and learning what makes them tick, as we go.

This is not a biography of my life. The book will cast a stone at a whole lot of observations and aspersions, and it's open to be disregarded in totality. I am just putting my thoughts in black and white. Join me in my thinking and observations if you have the energy and the time, as I generalise a lot about social things that come to my mind.

2

BRIEF BACKGROUND OF A BLACK TOWNSHIP CHILD

In a black township environment, going to school is seen as a way out of harsh poverty. It is also seen as a sign of intellect when the child is doing well or can speak fluent English. Reality has shown that school is never the way out of poverty nor is it an accumulation of intelligence. Knowledge including skill, must be learnt out of school. The first lessons a child in the township learns is to be street smart. This includes the skill of knowing when to run when you see danger, like being robbed, or never being naïve. The art of gambling with dice, marbles, and cards including the famous one called *Zwipi*. I will not define it but attempt to explain it. Someone spins a coin and hides the result in the palm of their hand. The bets are made by those in the circle who attempt to guess which side of the coin will be facing up when it is revealed. There are losers and winners. Sore losers will raise their objection by what we called *sghurughuru* back then, where they grab everything they lost including other people's money. This ended in chaos and fights.

One wonders why such an observation is necessary. This is what has shaped most kids my age from the township. And yes, we obviously had games to play which will take too much time to explain but, I will write them as we used to call them, and for ease of reference I will explain them with a footnote. These were games such as chigaco or *bathi*, *diketo*, *morabaraba*, scotch, draught, topo, *stena* (with marbles), *umgusha, ludo, kite, keti* (sling), car-making, soccer and others I might have forgotten to mention.

All these games had the potential for money to be involved and obviously chaos and fights were always imminent. Teamwork was critical to succeed in some of these games, while others were individual games, but all competitive. Wits and skills were observed from such games which no amount of school learning could prepare you for. Bullying was rife and boys in particular were subjected to huge beatings by most girls at those young ages. Disputable currently when we see the strife women have to endure at the hands of males when at one time a girl child was actually stronger than a boy child and smarter than boys, even at normal schooling.

The background I've described, was purely to elaborate how as kids we were free to do whatever and think whatever. Obviously with lots of boundaries and one-way discipline of a wet dish cloth or *skroplap* if you were lucky, but when the luck run out, belt, stick, shoe, tree branch or the palm of the hand on the behind, with some wicked parents who would use serious Mike Tyson punches to knock the sense out of freedom of speech and ill-discipline. Basically, corporal punishment was legal but today it is illegal. I can bet that a huge percentage of parents my age still dish out that kind of discipline, cause wow, that was a language we understood and the assumption is that our kids will understand it. This normally ends in serious opinions from the current generation that will shock our ancestors to quit their graves and relocate.

I have to admit that a thin line had to be drawn with the beatings. It helped some of us escape early death and jail. Others were not so lucky and were beaten to the point where they hated their parents or guardians. Is it a good or bad thing? I will let you be the judge but know what the law says.

All or most of the games we played back then had an element of teamwork, competition, money, street smart, and skills. I have heard some people say they learnt a lot about investing through playing monopoly but for me, I learnt *fokol* (nothing) from monopoly except trying to win and the fact that it was one long game. The tough life of a black child forces them to try hard to win no matter what. Survival is also key for a black child. We had a lot of trial-and error learning.

We actually made our own cars. The joy of finding parts and designing the car, shaping it and bringing it to life always surpassed the actual driving of it. Competition was very tight, and those who mastered the skill of car making, made a lot of money by selling them. That was entrepreneurship and innovation combined. We played and had real friends not just school friends. Playing inside the house was forbidden as we would dirty the house or yard. We were chased outside and encountered other risks like bad neighbours who would simply not spare us for making a noise.

We had encounters with abusers who molested boys. Some boys were not very lucky to escape their claws and would never want to tell that tale. That's how we knew words like *matanyula* (molestation of boys). We would keep such things very quiet and carry the hate till we were teenagers and exact a bitter revenge on those who did that with utter bemusement from the community.

We had concepts and terms like cheese-boy. That was reserved for any child who seemed to have a better life than all of us. They mostly had parents who worked or had a spaza shop. Cheese- boys would have all the nice toys including bicycles. We learnt how to ride the bicycle by paying a fee to the cheese-boy, however, they had to also like you to conclude such a transaction. Television was foreign, and those who had it, made us watch and asked for a fee such as buying floor polish to clean the house.

We used to collect empty bottles to trade with bottle collectors who drove around in a car or bakkie full of slap chips (we called them *shwamshwams* or Simba chips). You gave them a bottle and they would pour you a cup of slap chips, depending on how big your bottle was. We used to call that car a banana *kaar*, to this day I don't know how such a name came about because there was never a banana in the car. When we were hungry we had our rescue 911 in Zone 1 Meadowlands called *malebese* (feeding scheme). They would give us bread and peanut butter with milk. I must say that was the last option but we went there regularly.

We grew up and became teenagers. With that came some daunting experiences for boys as there were no cellphones. We had to approach young ladies to express our love. That was one thing that would make boys sweat with fear and become the laughing stock of other boys. Names such as *uyasha, une gwababa* or *une nyoni* (you are burning or scared), the worst one was 'you eat too much *skopas* — the sweet coloured popcorn sold on the streets) were common. To this day, I never understood why they said *skopas* caused fear of women, while they were such a hunger quencher and very tasty, I must say.

The ladies were fierce and unapproachable, they would put you in your place instantly especially if they didn't like you. This is where a lot of boys started practising violence against women. Being told where to get off created much laughter among our boy peers and the boy would retaliate by slapping the young lady. Women have always been great communicators from an early age and that created fools out of boys. A question like, 'Why do you love me?' from a woman would result in utter rubbish from an already panicked boy, or attempted poetry that would win the lady's heart. As a young man you learn that women actually know who they like; don't just go and approach anyone without seeing the signs.

Some topics were off limits with parents. Sex was a serious taboo to discuss with parents. Any explicit act that you saw on TV watching with parents always resulted in you being sent to make tea or coffee. Any chuckling while being systematically dismissed would result in a question that you are not supposed to answer if you had mastered the art of survival. That's how we learnt that not all truths should be told unless you are today's child. Other topics were freely discussed to ensure spine-chilling experiences. Topics such as witchcraft, *tikoloshis*, and the most dangerous among them definitely damaged our sub-conscience, and I never understood why we were subjected to it.

Those who understand, know the level of independence one needed to survive growing up. Times have changed drastically compared to back then but the concepts and mentality of the black child have not changed much. This is what inspired these writings: to ask questions of the black mind, to challenge the status quo; do things differently, to introspect on what we could call factory faults of being born black.

For instance, a young black girl plays with dolls and dreams of a family set-up that is peaceful, while a young black boy will play with cars and guns. Marriage and the family set-up were entrenched in the young black girl's mind, while violence and the fast life or aiming to impress were what young black boys grew up wanting. The first thing a young black man will think of when he gets a job or makes money, will be a car, clothes, fun and womanising. A young black woman will be looking for stability and making sure she looks as beautiful as she dreamed she would. How is this important? In a nutshell, kids are shaped by their exposure, background and most importantly, learn by observation. Any parent or guardian trying to teach a child, needs to know that walking the talk will play a big role for that child.

> *"Children have never been very good at listening to their elders but have never failed to imitate them."*
> **—James A. Baldwin**

3

THE OUTDATED EDUCATION SYSTEM

A brief history of education

This detailed history was explained by Dr Peter Gray:

"In relation to the biological history of our species, schools are very recent institutions. For hundreds of thousands of years, before the advent of agriculture, we lived as hunter-gatherers. The strong drives in children to play and explore presumably came about, during our evolution as hunter-gatherers, to serve the needs of education. Adults in hunter-gatherer cultures allowed children almost unlimited freedom to play and explore on their own because they recognised that those activities are children's natural ways of learning.

"With the rise of agriculture, and later of industry, children became forced labourers. Play and exploration were suppressed. Wilfulness, which had been a virtue, became a vice that had to be beaten out of children.

"The invention of agriculture, beginning 10,000 years ago in some parts of the world and later in other parts, set in motion a whirlwind of change in people's ways of living. The hunter-gatherer way of life had been skill-intensive and knowledge-intensive, but not labour-intensive. To be effective hunters and gatherers, people had to acquire a vast knowledge of the plants and animals on which they depended and of the landscapes within which they foraged. They also had to develop great skill in crafting and using the tools of hunting and gathering. They had to be able to take initiative and be creative in finding foods and tracking game. However, they did not have to work long hours; and the work they did was exciting, not dreary. Anthropologists have reported that the hunter-gatherer groups they studied did not distinguish between work and play – essentially all of life was understood as play.

"Agriculture gradually changed all that. With agriculture, people could produce more food, which allowed them to have more children. Agriculture also allowed people (or forced people) to live in permanent dwellings, where their crops were planted, rather than live a nomadic life, and this in turn allowed people to accumulate property. But these changes occurred at a great cost in labour. While hunter-gatherers skilfully harvested what nature had grown, farmers had to plough, plant, cultivate, tend their flocks, and so on. Successful farming required long hours of relatively unskilled, repetitive labour, much of which could be done by children. With larger families, children had to work in the fields to help feed their younger siblings, or they had to work at home to help care for those siblings. Children's lives changed gradually from the free pursuit of their own interests to increasingly more time spent at work that was required to serve the rest of the family.

"Agriculture and the associated ownership of land and accumulation of property also created clear status differences. People who did not own land became dependent on those who did. Also, landowners discovered that they could increase their own wealth by getting other people to work for them. Systems of slavery and other forms of servitude developed. Those with wealth could become even wealthier with the help of others who depended on them for survival. All this culminated with feudalism in the Middle Ages, when society became steeply hierarchical, with a few kings and lords at the top and masses of slaves and serfs at the bottom. Now the lot of most people, children included, was servitude. The principal lessons that children had to learn were obedience, suppression of their own will, and the show of reverence toward lords and masters. A rebellious spirit could well result in death. In the Middle Ages, lords and masters had no qualms about physically beating children into submission.

"With the rise of industry and of a new bourgeoisie class, feudalism gradually subsided, but this did not immediately improve the lives of most children. Business owners, like landowners, needed labourers and could profit by extracting as much work from them as possible with as little compensation as possible. Everyone knows of the exploitation that followed and still exists in many parts of the world. People, including young children, worked most of their waking hours, seven days a week, in beastly conditions, just to survive. The labour of children was moved from fields, where there had at least been sunshine, fresh air, and some opportunities to play, into dark, crowded, dirty factories.

"In summary, for several thousand years after the advent of agriculture, the education of children was, to a considerable degree, a matter squashing their wilfulness in order to make them good labourers. A good child was an obedient child, who suppressed his or her urge to play and explore and dutifully carried out the orders of adult masters. Such education, fortunately, was never fully successful. The human instincts to play and explore are so powerful that they can never be fully beaten out of a child.

"For various reasons, some religious and some secular, the idea of universal, compulsory education arose and gradually spread. Education was understood as inculcation.

"As industry progressed and became somewhat more automated, the need for child labour declined in some parts of the world. The idea began to spread that childhood should be a time for learning, and schools for children were developed as places of learning. The idea and practice of universal, compulsory public education developed gradually in Europe, from the early 16th century on into the 19th. It was an idea that had many supporters, who all had their own agendas concerning the lessons that children should learn.

"Employers in industry saw schooling as a way to create better workers. To them, the most crucial lessons were punctuality, following directions, tolerance for long hours of tedious work, and a minimal ability to read and write. From their point of view (though they may not have put it this way), the duller the subjects taught in schools the better. As nations gelled and became more centralised, national leaders saw schooling as a means of creating good patriots and future soldiers. To them, the crucial lessons were about the glories of the fatherland, the wondrous achievements and moral virtues of the nation's founders and leaders, and the necessity to defend the nation from evil forces elsewhere.

"Into this mix we must add reformers who truly cared about children, whose messages may ring sympathetically in our ears today. These are people who saw schools as places for protecting children from the damaging forces of the outside world and for providing children with the moral and intellectual grounding needed to develop into upstanding, competent adults. But they too had their agenda for what children should learn. Children should learn moral lessons and disciplines, such as Latin and mathematics, that would exercise their minds and turn them into scholars.

"So, everyone involved in the founding and support of schools had a clear view about what lessons children should learn in school. Quite correctly, nobody believed that children left to their own devices, even in a rich setting for learning, would all learn just exactly the lessons that they (the adults) deemed to be so important. All of them saw schooling as inculcation, the implanting of certain truths and ways of thinking into children's minds. The only known method of inculcation, then as well as now, is forced repetition and testing for memory of what was repeated. Brainwashing to say the least.

"Repetition and memorisation of lessons is tedious work for children, whose instincts urge them constantly to play freely and explore the world on their own. Just as children did not adapt readily to labouring in fields and factories, they did not adapt readily to schooling. This was no surprise to the adults involved. By this point in history, the idea that children's own wilfulness had any value was pretty well forgotten. Everyone assumed that to make children learn in school the children's wilfulness would have to be beaten out of them. Punishments of all sorts were understood as intrinsic to the educational process. In some schools, children were permitted certain periods of play (recess), to allow them to let off steam; but play was not considered to be a vehicle of learning. In the classroom, play was the enemy of learning.

"The brute force methods long used to keep children on task on the farm or in the factory were transported into schools to make children learn. Some of the underpaid, ill-prepared schoolmasters were clearly sadistic. In recent times, the methods of schooling have become less harsh, but basic assumptions have not changed. Learning continues to be defined as children's work, and power-assertive means are used to make children do that work.

"In the 19th and 20th centuries, public schooling gradually evolved toward what we all recognise today as conventional schooling. The methods of discipline became more humane, or at least less corporal; the lessons became more secular; the curriculum expanded, as knowledge expanded, to include an ever-growing list of subjects; and the number of hours, days, and years of compulsory schooling increased continuously. School gradually replaced fieldwork, factory work, and domestic chores as the child's primary job. Just as adults put in their eight-hour day at their place of employment, children today put in their six-hour day at school, plus another hour or more of homework, and often more hours of lessons outside of school. Over time, children's lives have become increasingly defined and structured by the school curriculum. Children now are almost universally identified by their grade in school, much as adults are identified by their job or career."

Is the current education system effective to challenge the needs of the changing world?

Attending school in the 80s and 90s was never a joy ride for those who understand the system we had to endure back then. We had education under the apartheid system which was never meant to develop and grow a black child to be a thinker or innovator. Nonetheless, innovation has never been a strong point of any educational system even now.

My education journey allowed me to see how educational inequality contributes to social and income inequality, thus creating a poverty cycle. The education system was built with a bias: bias in deciding where to direct funds, bias in the material chosen to teach, and bias in the school's location. It makes all the difference in the world if your neighbourhood is wealthy or poor. The bias is dependent upon 'the haves and have nots' mentality, and this bias determines student success.

There is a study that says intelligence has nine different descriptions which can be connected to the brain. Visual (picture smart), linguistic (word smart), logical (number/reasoning smart), kinaesthetic (body smart), naturalist (nature smart), musical (sound smart), existential (life smart), interpersonal (people smart) and intra-personal (self-smart). It is very difficult to find one person possessing all of them but it is never strange when one has them.

This clearly shows us that no one is actually a fool, idiot or *domkop*. They just possess a different kind of intelligence, while we judge each other with only the school way of doing things. Albert Einstein said: "If you judge a fish by its ability to climb a tree, it will live its whole life thinking it's stupid." He further said: "Education is what remains after one has forgotten what one has learned in school," and "It is a miracle that curiosity survives formal education," and finally "The only thing that interferes with my learning is my education."

In a post-industrial world, education may require an equally bold rethink. It might mean more comprehensive adult education, or regular retraining, to keep skills sharp as old jobs disappear and new ones appear that require vastly different responsibilities. Or it may involve integrating technology to create more personalised learning experiences.

Modern captains of industry take more of a hands-off approach to education. They complain about skill shortages, but don't offer the same leadership and willingness to fight vested interests as their predecessors. Maybe it is time that they did.

By ignoring the individual qualities, strengths, and interests of students, our society has failed to use schools to support students' strengths and passions and instead has forced them to follow arbitrary tasks largely aimed at training students to pass tests. They are cramped together in a class and expected to conform as if they are not individuals with unique qualities that need to be nurtured.

Despite the advancements of the past 50 years, schools continue to teach without the aid of technology. Even with the abundance of information we can access, our schools continue to demand discipline and restrict out-of-the-box thinking, leaving little or no room for technological teaching methods and innovation within the classroom. If the world around us changes and we do not, how are our students going to be prepared for the jobs of the future – largely technology-based, non-traditional careers? The current education system is teaching us outdated skills designed for the industrial era and ignoring modern history; a modern history that will dictate the career paths of current students.

The struggle in most South African areas, predominantly townships and rural areas is dire. Before they struggle with the quality of teaching, they have to contend with lack of teachers, sanitation, food, textbooks and schools themselves. The government seems to have an idea from Statistics South Africa of what skills are lacking in industry and areas that need attention but they have no clue how to resolve all the problems. To date, we have a lot of unemployed graduates with qualifications that are deemed irrelevant or in over supply.

Many parents have been left disappointed with the current education system or schools, as it seems they are designed for parents. Parents find themselves doing more school work, and children have no time at all to be children. After hours of being at school, children come home to more schooling. There is no innovation possible due to these restrictions. There is lack of development for talented children in areas such as sports and arts unless they attend affluent schools and pay exorbitant fees. This is the reality for the masses in South Africa.

Can something be done to improve the current situation?

Educational inequity is holding our students back from reaching their full potential and holding the younger generations back from receiving the best education possible. In holding students back, we are depriving future society of the best foundation possible for a better world.

Education should be treated as an investment into the future of our country, investors should not hesitate to do their part in planning ahead and securing the future of a nation. As adults, constituents, educators, lawmakers, parents, and lifelong learners, we are responsible for the education our children receive.

The children we are subjecting to a poorly designed education system will be the ones leading our country. What do we want the future of our country to look like? What should our educational system look like in order to achieve this? These are the questions we must ask. As patrons of the process, we can no longer look the other way. We can no longer ignore the political process. We must make our voices heard.

Technology should be used to advance the way students learn information particularly because it enables individualised learning, leading to student satisfaction and productivity. With 21st century technology, we have more opportunity and ability to create change than ever before. We have the power to shape how we think the world should operate, and so far, we have not taken advantage of that opportunity. We can no longer allow our children to suffer through poorly-funded educational measures or selectively pick which students learn without the proper resources.

We need solution- driven education to resolve the current and future possible problems. Pandemics like Covid-19 would not have caught us by surprise had the industry captains and governments listened to the warnings issued five years ago. Investment in research and young vibrant brains could actually speed up a lot of solutions. We have innovators trying to invest in space travel but the ground work education doesn't correspond with such innovations.

If we can change how we approach education, we have the potential to decrease the achievement gap and change the future of socioeconomic inequality. We are all human. We all deserve an equal education. Let's stand up to teach our students the importance of learning, develop a culture around education, and teach all students, despite race, gender, ethnicity, and socioeconomic class the skills they need to tackle the problems of the future. Let us take a stand and voice what we need our government to focus on and to invest in the correct education methods and system.

> *"A man's mind, stretched by new ideas, may never return to its original dimensions."* —**Oliver Wendell Holmes Jr.**

> *"Education is the passport to the future, for tomorrow belongs to those who prepare for it today."* —**Malcolm X**

> *"If you think education is expensive, try ignorance."* —**Andy McIntyre**

4

EMANCIPATION OF
A BLACK MIND

Why a big word like emancipation? I don't know, it just felt appropriate, but it simply means freedom or liberation. The heading simply means free the black mind.

So then, how do we free a black mind? My observations always lead me to one shocking idea, that we have serious factory faults that we need to address before we can even talk 'emancipation'. In general, black people have the short-term mindset of living a comfortable life. Get a job, sell this for a profit and survive, get this and that so that you can be respected or any other strange thing like *baloyi ba mpone* (witches, see my success. Tupac Shakur said in one of his songs, 'picture me rollin'). Even a well-educated black person will cry about not having a job, which clearly shows why being street smart from childhood has lost us. The survival instinct of winning at whatever it takes has eluded us.

Let me use an example of stokvels, a concept most black people in our country are familiar with. What I know about most stokvels is that a group of people agree verbally or in writing to contribute monthly, an agreed fixed amount. This money is saved in a bank account with a few signatories (the integrity of stokvel signatories is a topic on its own with sadness and funny stories). The savings are used for different purposes, be it burial assistance, year-end groceries or sharing out the money at an agreed time. I will not dwell on the administration of stokvels, nor all the risks and rewards of it as I'm not skilled or knowledgeable enough to do that, nor am I a registered financial service provider. However, what has touched my observation is that a culture of saving is there and observed strictly in the stokvel.

What puzzles me is that, when the time comes to share this money, particularly the wicked December period. I say wicked because in my observation, it is the time when spending recklessly seems to be an acceptable norm for most black families who have little or more to spend. How does this help in the emancipation of a black mind? Let's look at the following analysis:

"Current estimates are that there are over 820 000 stokvels in the country with a combined membership of 11.4 million people, handling over R44 billion per annum. Most of the money is paid out monthly, to individuals, who spend it on consumables, food and groceries. And that is where it often ends." (www.iol.co.za)

"In-depth research into 36 stokvels revealed that the majority of members were not aware of how the money they generated could be invested or put to better use. The money received from members usually goes into a savings club account at a bank, where it is known as a 'lazy deposit' as the amount gains little to no interest and banks are able to invest the money profitably, all with no benefit to the stokvel members." (Rudzani Mulaudzi)

"Next to banks, big retailers are the other real beneficiaries of the way stokvels currently operate – cashing in on the money deposited, which often translates into bulk buying once a year. Many stokvel members club together to buy groceries, sending trucks to hypermarkets to buy items which are perhaps reduced by as little as 1% in price. A group can easily spend R200, 000 on groceries." (Rudzani Mulaudzi)

The three paragraphs above may lead one to ask why black people are still so poor? Well from an observation, we are simply consumers not investors. Our goals are for short-term comforts in nature. A social media joke said: "Only black people will contribute to buy a factory and turn it into a church, then go to the same church and pray for jobs." That says a lot about our mindset. We can easily run to get rich quick schemes, WhatsApp stokvels, even run around to recruit more people so we don't lose alone but can never do the same to invest in legit businesses or support an emerging entre-preneur. Where have you seen someone with knowledge of how to be rich recruiting people? I will let you think for a while. I can never understand such factory fault mentality but nonetheless these are our people.

We always cry that we bring each other down as black people, and we don't get along, but the reality is that we actually don't have the mindset for long-term planning. If we did get along, then the banks wouldn't be collecting R44 billion a year from 11 million South Africans on stokvels alone. In 2019 elections, about 17 million people voted – only the ruling party obtained 10 million votes across the country. Imagine what the power of R44 billion a year and 11 million people behind it would do for this country and the black people. If only the goals were not short-term orientated but dynamic enough to conquer and rewrite history. I'm bringing this to your attention, not to start a revolution but to suggest a mindset clean-up for the black child.

Another shocking introspecting article I read said: "The taxi industry in South Africa continues to grow despite a tough economy. It's now worth about R50 billion a year, with 69% of South African households using minibus taxis. Transaction Capital reported that its SA Taxi business, which finances, sells, and insures minibus taxis, grew its half-year headline earnings by almost a third. Loans to taxi operators jumped 14% to more than R10.1 billion. SA Taxi finances some 650 minibus taxis every month, and it has 30,000 operators on its books." (Business Insider)

Now a R50 billion industry a year with 69% of SA households using minibus taxis should trigger a few concerns. Who benefits from the R10,1 billion in loans? None of the taxi associations appear in the list of top 10 shareholders of Transaction Capital. None of the black employees are in the management of the company with the exception of one independent non-executive director from 10 managers. This is an embarrassment to all taxi associations and taxi owners for their lack of vision. What makes matters worse is that 43% of all assassinations in South Africa are related to the taxi industry. With the power of loans and income generation, the taxi industry should be a serious force within the business world as they can influence transportation. When they stop business, industries suffer. But what is disturbing is that they cannot get along where it should matter most; they do though for strikes and disturbing the economy to get grievances heard. They should have airlines, trains, trucks etc...in fact they should be running Uber as well.

Malcom X said, "We need more light about each other. Light creates understanding, understanding creates love, love creates patience and patience creates unity." He further quotes that, "You have to be very careful introducing the truth to the black man who has never previously heard the truth about himself. The black brother is so brainwashed that he may reject the truth when he first hears it. You have to drop it on him [a little] at a time and wait a while to let it sink in before advancing to the next step."

Stokvels alone can own a bank/s or grocery shops. One may argue that we had a VBS bank, which is notoriously known for falling flat due to factors known to us via the media. The truth is that the goals and objectives were not in solidarity for long-term ownership, where the contributors could actually select signatories or people who run the bank. The groceries we buy in December with the stokvel money are the backbone of sustaining grocery shops that embarrass our people with low wages/ salaries and bad working conditions, yet the same employees contribute to the stokvel. It leaves a bitter taste in my mouth to think that we can't buy shares in those grocery shops and appoint our people to be at the helm of decision making through the power of voting in directors.

We grew up designing our own toy cars but to this day South Africa has no car proudly made by us, yet we are sold a pacification that BBBEE has chased skilled engineers out of our country. How coy for such statements to be made, when the reality is well known that back then our careers were limited to teaching, nursing or police officers. We innovated games to play yet despite technology, I haven't seen one of those games being designed to capture the new generation we are raising. Yet we have a lot of so-called IT gurus who are black but are busy in jobs making money for the same organisations that don't recognise them. (I'm pricking a lot of souls and I can see a lot of unhappiness and excuses).

One thing I admire about black people in my country, is their spontaneous nature of organising anything, or mob revolution. We can wake up without a plan but end up having a wild party (fun), money spent, hashtag YOLO (you only live once). This to me says we can actually organise anything we set our minds to. You will be asleep and when you wake up, there is a huge barricade on the roads and our people have mobilised to toyi-toyi (strike or protest) to express their displeasure on one or other matter pertaining to government, or an ill committed in the society. When it comes to bad financial schemes, you will realise that even the hermits can communicate eloquently and try to market the scheme yet fail to market their ideas.

The total dependency on our government by our people has made a lot of minds redundant. We have so called entrepreneurs who actually are not entrepreneurs but hustlers with government links and connections. Not that it's wrong to depend on government. They supply and deliver for the state for years, yet they don't own any logistics company, or a factory to produce or mass import. All they do is feel entitled to what government must be doing to assist them. How many times must one be assisted before they can evolve? The grant system has clouded our people's brains to a point that they seek loopholes on how to defraud the same system that should be helping the needy.

We have people appointed to government portfolios who have never studied for them or never studied at all but we expect that there will be proper administration. We live in an era where politicians are rich beyond imagination yet they are servants of the people who are extremely poor. There is a lack of united political direction that will sing a tune to ensure the economy is restored back into the hands of the masses, instead of the pockets of the few elite and connected.

You may ask, why can't we unite to form a common goal that will sustain us and our future generation? I honestly don't know; maybe *ba re loyile* (maybe we are bewitched). That term of being bewitched has been our sad corner to hide in for any failures we encounter. Why are we so religious yet don't even dominate industries that generate income for everyone? Can we ever unite to conquer and be independent as Africans? I believe we can, or I hope we do or let us at least encourage our children to unite and conquer.

Can we make our money circulate within black businesses before it goes out?

The concept of Ubuntu has disappeared and been replaced by greed, laziness, entitlement, jealousy, selfishness, pride, slander and a public display of personal achievements right in the face of the poor and needy. We have built fences in our yards that will embarrass a talented athletic high jumper. We move to the suburbs in closed secure gated areas and tell our relatives they need to make an appointment to come see us, but when newly adopted friends come visit they are more than welcome or even known by the security personnel. We attend churches with passion yet learn nothing from the teachings of the bible, like loving one another. Are we doomed?

Our townships have been taken over by foreign spaza shops right in front of our eyes, including a whole lot of businesses in our towns. Their businesses are not doing anything different from what an ordinary passionate South African can do with the right support. If a South African can be assisted to open a spaza shop or any business instead of taking money pumped into grants, we can solve some of the unemployment problems in the country. We cannot go into any African country and open a business in the local townships, yet in South Africa everything is possible and easy. When such is raised, its xenophobic. I'm raising our mindset to shake things up, let's own our businesses, let's support them.

We have so much that we can utilise and commercialise at our disposal yet we have to wait for it to be converted into a product by industries and then buy it. A simple *impepho* (liquorice plant) which most households use, is not yet commercialised by us to ensure that we farm it, package it and re-sell it on the shelves of the supermarkets. To get *impepho* you must go into some freaky shady place instead of a business market created by government to support indigenous products. If you go to Takealot.com, you will find them being sold including soap bars made from them, but none of the products are proudly made by black South Africans who consume or prescribe them for traditional healing.

Medical cannabis has been allowed to be sold legally but instead of obtaining land via stokvel money and commercialising this big opportunity, we are only comfortable to look sexy smoking it. While we know very well that there is a huge industry for it, especially if it can be commercialised. One could argue, why am I not doing anything about it? Well I'm writing what I observe, and this is my skill. I'm not an entrepreneur but I know this might ignite a whole lot of entrepreneurs who have resorted to limiting their ideas to government tenders. Out of 10 top construction companies, only one is proudly black woman-owned. But we see those tender-preneurs flashing cars and money daily on social media.

Our country is hot but we are not using solar energy or capitalising on it, especially with the failures of our main electricity supplier who is not worth mentioning by name. Our government should already be directing investments in education and business to ensure this massive solar energy is realised by our people. They would rather bring foreign companies who will come in as wolves in sheep's clothing saying they are investing in our country. An investor seeks returns, always.

We have a whole lot of individual success stories of black business that we must praise, support and motivate. If you can afford a Gucci, Versace or Louis Vuitton, what makes it difficult to afford Amaxhosa, Bathu, Drip, DM Bespoke Suits or any other proudly South African brands and businesses? If you tell me it's about taste and choice, then I say to you, just go buy it and support it because these are our brothers and sisters making a difference. Let us be proud of our achievements. Let us circulate our money at least five times into black hands before it goes outside.

I know I must mind my own business and let us enjoy our hard-earned money. The truth is that we have to change our mindset and start creating a foundation for our kids to at least start on equal footing with most kids of other races. We know that our salaries, for those who are lucky to earn them, are not enough. As I'm writing this, the world is faced with a pandemic called COVID-19. It has exposed a lot of our people and governments to the harsh inequalities. A lot of business people came to face the ugly truth that they have been living from hand to mouth unable to sustain themselves.

"If you wake up deciding what you want to give versus what you're going to get, you become a more successful person. In other words, if you want to make money, you have to help someone else make money." **—Russell Simmons**

"I built a conglomerate and emerged the richest black man in the world in 2008 but it didn't happen overnight. It took me 30 years to get to where I am today. Youths of today aspire to be like me but they want to achieve it overnight. It's not going to work. To build a successful business, you must start small and dream big. In the journey of entrepreneurship, tenacity of purpose is supreme." **—Aliko Dangote**

5

THE PRIVATE AND PUBLIC-SECTOR WORK ENVIRONMENT

"The average annual earning among black people was R6 009 in 2006 and R9 186 in 2015, while the figures for the white population were R77 308 in 2006 and R100 205 in 2015." (STATS SA)

Let me share what I read about Elon Musk. If you don't know him please Google him. At the age of 12 he developed and sold a code of a BASIC-based video game called Blaster. This was in South Africa, and at that age, approximately in 1983 considering his current age of 49, when the rand dollar exchange was just R1.12. He sold that code for $500, which is currently equivalent to $1 316.47 or R33 766.66, taking into consideration an adjusted inflation rate of 2.65%. Why is this important to mention? I'm just showing you how the playing fields are not so easy for most black people. That much money was never seen by our parents in a year's salary in 1983; needless to say, most black people don't even know it in today's world of 2020.

The above figures were in a Stats SA article and I thought let me bring it here, just to raise the mindset and probably make you continue reading all the gibberish in my brain that I'm putting in black and white.

I have experience of working in the private sector, and public sector, also as a hustler (in terms of buying and selling goods). Now some hustlers define themselves as business people, while others have registered companies and businesses but still remain hustlers. Their venture never evolves into a business that expands, creates jobs and grows big. Why am I mentioning this? Because there is huge difference between a business person and a hustler. When you hustle to make ends meet or supplement your income to put food on your table or whatever reason, you have a different mindset to someone who wants to be a business person, wealthy/rich or successful. That's just my observation though, as I have been a hustler before and I know I didn't want any responsibilities of hiring anyone or paying anyone for something I can do. I deemed that stress. I fortunately went to school and am one of the lucky ones to be employed. I suffer from the same fate most employees suffer from – a salary comfort zone.

• Semi-skilled Independent Black Workers (private contractors)

Is it me alone struggling with our independent black skilled workers or am I just biased? Let me not even get to the stories on such matters of our beloved brothers and sisters who provide so much of the help we need so desperately. From the disappearing of clothes, tools, unfinished plumbing or shady mechanics, the list of the disappointments is endless. Some of the challenges are caused by us, we negotiate the price too much, get shady work and then complain.

The current environment and time exposed most working families to require help in terms of running households. Gone are the days when our mothers would run the whole household, from cleaning and laundry to gardening and end up forgetting themselves, let alone receive any recognition at all from family members. The current norm and economy require everyone to pull their weight in bringing income to the household, and therefore we end up needing helpers. This has led many foolish and wicked men to judge women differently if they can't cook or clean, while surprisingly the same man cannot even fry an egg or clean his underwear. (Yes, I'm generalising).

Now the help we hire is totally different to what we are used to or assume how they should be. For some of us, our mothers were domestic workers, and we heard stories of how they were treated and yet they endured and woke up to go to work only to get a bonus of groceries and old clothes. The current help has rights and trust me they know their rights, just like you as an employee has rights. In a formal industry, be it private sector or public sector there are rules and regulations and codes of conduct, while the informal workers have no such luxuries.

The mistake most black people make, is to hire a helper for house work and expect them to behave like a formal industry employee with pension, medical aid and other benefits. Someone in your household becomes a part of the family and should reasonably be treated and handled with extreme care for you to have joy and comfort that your house will be safe when you are not around. They interact with your children if you have them and are critical in ensuring their safety, but they are never a substitute for your absence. The domestic help you hire also has a life outside your environment. Their life must be respected and valued.

- ## The Private Sector environment

In the private sector environment, my observation is obscured by the political bias that exists towards black people. I have observed how quickly young white employees climb the corporate ladder compared to equally competent black employees. How much education must a black person have to even be considered for a supervisory position? On the other hand, Caucasians can get away with enthusiasm; attitude and all rubbish reasons are imposed on a black child.

The unfortunate part is that you cannot fight the system, and if you do the system will make sure it spews you out. In general, a black employee doesn't just have to show up at work but has to constantly prove to everyone that he is a good and reliable employee. Merely reporting that you are sick can be met with a verbal warning if not written, while for the other race, there will be exceptions. If you raise such observations, you will be lucky to get a performance bonus, promotion, or any recognition. Now this might seem like a racist observation, well it is, though it's the systematic kind of racism. For a black employee to be in a senior position, they must be exceptional or lick a lot of human behinds, but for a white employee, a little education if any, and their privilege sets them apart.

A black employee can work hard and ignore all politics, be liked by bosses, and grow in rank, yet they will face one major problem. Other black people. Instead of your fellow black people celebrating your success, you will experience the most excruciating criticism and hatred beyond imagination. This is purely based on the in-depth knowledge that only one or few black people will reach that level, and now when you are the chosen one, you have left a bitter taste around their dreams and ambitions of growth in many of your fellowmen's mouths. We don't think beyond that position.

Our mindset doesn't set the target of rising to the boardroom, because we subconsciously know it is very hard to get that far. If one ever gets that far, we celebrate like a pit-bull smiling, wondering how you got there, what did you do to get there, which politician you are affiliated with, who did she sleep with, who you know or what you studied at school?

The salary comparison between races in the private sector will leave anyone with a sane mind confused and disgusted. This has only made the fights worse between black employees as they end up comparing each other's salaries but in silence, as the private sector has mastered the art of hiding such things and making them an offence. In the public sector, salaries are publicly known, making fights of a different nature.

Innovation in the private sector is encouraged, but rewards are not so big, hence we have to this day a company case of a former employee who came with the 'Please call me' invention which is still dragging and the individual has not been paid. This has discouraged many black employees to express their talent as they know, someone will be appointed on top of them to run their ideas. (intrapreneur: an employee who proposes and manages a project within the company in which he works. He bears a moral risk but a non-financial risk).

The share incentive schemes are reserved only for the elite few, as a form of retaining them in the company for a very long time. This is just another form of capture, as no one will afford your skills outside. That big fat pay cheque makes sure you preach their gospel instead of the emancipation and development of the black race, who is probably a major consumer of the product or service being sold.

My writing might seem to be discrediting the private sector to those who think they have benefitted immensely from it. I therefore ask, what have you done for other black employees to reach your level? What have you done for your community? What have you done for your friends and family? A white child attends their parent's employment and learns the trade and skills from them at a young age, and they end up even knowing the right people to a point that years later they join the same corporation. Black children will not be tolerated to accumulate such knowledge as they are considered unruly, to say the least. Like I said, yes, I can generalise. This is just my observation.

The sad reality is that some or the majority of the revenue generated by the private sector is from the black population. I stand to be corrected. Yet the same black people cannot be trusted to manage those companies and come up with better innovative ideas for the products they consume. When you go to most universities in the country, you will find a lot of black students, but sadly the working class will subject them to mere subordinate status or clerks. Most will see a pay cheque over R10 000 for the first time and think they have arrived. They will forget their goals and ambitions so quickly and start to face reality when debts and so called black tax comes to play (I don't know who came up with the term black tax, but reality says a black person takes care of his family and parents; black tax connotation is nonsense to me. You are doing an Ubuntu thing that is supposed to be done. And yes, I know you don't owe them anything). The playing fields are not level for a lot of black employees, hence we celebrate things like being the first to buy a car, a home or go to university or be the first to do something.

The black employee is currently immersed in debt, which causes a lot of strain on their growth potential and translates to abuses and possibly malfunctioning families (I know a huge number of South Africans debt ratio is around 70% so relax this is not about all of you). I'm extreme I know, because not only debt contributes to such matters.

What makes the debt matter worse is that even the unemployed have huge debt, so they will enter the working world with debt, if they are lucky to re-enter with the current economic conditions and lack of clear political direction. I'm tempted to use the common term 'middle class' but the way things are in 2020, there is no longer a middle class. We all suffer the same fate, and many are running to the Unemployment Insurance Fund due to the corona pandemic that has closed many companies.

The private sector is failing to teach its employees about financial management, lifestyle, education and development. The most prized asset in any organisation is its employees, but in truth we know value is placed on profitability. The triple bottom line reporting is for compliance sake. The majority of black employees don't save or have nothing to save after what they earn. The financial gurus will tell us to have at least three times our salary saved for emergencies. That's just a pipe dream for many employees.

We need to see programmes that will develop long serving and or qualified black employees to executive positions. Let the playing fields be fair and not be race or gender based like it is right now. When these facts are raised, they are totally denied. Statements like 'you should be grateful you have a job' are common and preached as if you don't add value as a black employee.

The private sector needs to look into itself and understand how much of the social ills it is creating. They can't be solely blamed though because some of the ills are self-created by us as black employees for senseless things that we must truly face and accept.

• **The Public-Sector Environment**

According to the government's *June 2014 Quarterly Employment Statistics (QES) survey*, there were 455,701 national government employees, a further 1,118,748 people working for provincial authorities, 311,361 people were employed by local authorities and 275,851 employees worked for '"other government institutions' like libraries, parks, zoos and education and training authorities. This adds up to a grand total of 2.161million civil servants.

Government remains the major employer in the country, while the private sector has Anglo American as the biggest employer, followed closely by Bidvest and then Shoprite. This is just information based and has nothing to do with my thinking.

The public sector is a highly regulated environment yet so controversial to many of our citizens who are breaking those regulations. There is minimal joy, to say the least, about the public sector if we are to be honest with each other. Be it national, provincial or local, all sectors are riddled with incompetence, failure of systems, lack of technology and innovation, politics and political and union interference, corruption, lack of efficiency and lack of consequences.

To counter all the bad taste in the government, they came up with the term *Batho Pele*. *Batho Pele*, is Sesotho and means 'People First'. It is an initiative that was launched in 1997 to transform the public service at all levels. Batho Pele was launched because democratic South Africa inherited a public service that was not people-friendly and lacked the skills and attitudes to meet the developmental challenges facing the country. In the struggle to transform the public service, the old culture had to be changed to ensure that people are served properly, that all staff work to their full capacity and treat state resources with respect. In other words, instead of looking for reasons why government cannot do something, they have to find better ways to deliver what people need.

It sounds so nice that such a principle exists in the public sector, yet there is so much unhappiness with the conduct of public servants. Twenty-six years later, the service has become an extreme nightmare. When you look into a list of top employers for 2020, only one state-owned entity appears which is ACSA, and to my surprise SAPS is on that list. I have no qualms about ACSA, as we know our airports function well with minimal accidents. I can never say the same about SAPS and I bet I'm not the only one who is totally unhappy with their conduct.

I started working in the public sector seven years ago and had to come to terms with the fact that profit is not a driver for performance. *Batho Pele* principles are known only for interview purposes but never practised. Entitlement mentality is a default among many public-sector employees. Consequence management or lack thereof is a major challenge, resulting in a false confidence among employees that a public servant cannot be fired. Union interference is big, and this is powered by a workforce of 2,1 million people. There are a whole lot of different kinds of employees within the public sector, and some contribute to the challenges the nation is facing, while some are assisting in service delivery. Political interference is a well-known undocumented law, which also results in vacancy fillings.

Government is a major purchaser of goods and services in the country but have never utilised that power to effectively stimulate the economy. I have stated that the public sector is highly regulated but rules are disobeyed so much that outcomes of Auditor General reports can always be predicted. Most regulations make no sense at all, yet compliance is pushed as a key thing. There is a disjuncture between service delivery and compliance with the regulations. Those who set rules and regulations for the operations of the public sector, seem to have no clue about the true state of operations on the ground and the plight of the communities.

COVID-19 has exposed the idea that government actually can deliver certain basic needs. The reality is that, a disaster had to happen so that rules and regulations could be overlooked and service delivery happen faster. With such speedy service there is always an element of greed and corruption. Just because something is not exposed, doesn't make it correct. For government to enhance service delivery, a need now arises to review all red tape. For example, a public tender process must be concluded in 90 days after closing of the public advertisement. Before the advert appears, it must be published in the Tender Bulletin. An order must be placed two weeks in advance. The advert must be in the public space for a minimum of 21 days. What this simply means is that to appoint a company to build a new road will take a maximum of 121 days. Trust the public-sector employee to drag this out to a point where they request an extension.

Something has to be done and speedily so to revive the public-sector environment. The public-sector environment has created a space for a lot of vulture companies which easily provide loans to the public-sector employees due to the fact that employee incomes are stable. The worst of this is that they have agreements with government institutions to deduct from employees' salaries for a meagre fee to the state. The state should be protecting its employees from such vultures but it's doing little. Enforced formal education should be a priority but it is not, but expensive short courses by private individuals who are milking the state is a norm. The state will promise communities houses for years and still fail to deliver due to red tape and corruption. Schools, some public hospitals and clinics have been closed, but the state is not generating income from such buildings or utilising them as offices for its massive workforce. The state would rather rent from private individuals (majority are not black) and reduce the money that could be spent on service delivery.

Any individual who has to wake up and go to a public-sector institution for assistance, be it health, licence renewal, school application, ID or passport application or any other service, can attest to the stress they have days before they embark on such a mission. A simple visit to a service delivery centre can turn into a nightmare and a long wait that will embarrass even a black church service that goes on for hours. The arrogance and nonchalant attitude of the officials assisting you will remind you why prayer or why meditation is essential.

The salaries of public servants have been modified though not to a point that will help curb corruption but are very competitive. Salaries are gazetted and publicised, so it is easy to estimate the salary of a public servant if you know their level. If there are increases, it will be across the board irrespective of work performance, at an agreed percentage at the bargaining councils. The big chunk of salaries gets eaten up by politicians who actually are not operational but simply political party mandate pushers. This creates more pressure in service delivery, whereby quality jobs and salaries cannot be offered to deserving employees as they are limited by the grading that is gazetted. Effort is never equal to reward, hence the nonchalant attitude of public servants.

I want to throw down the gauntlet to highlight some loopholes as government is crying out about employment creation. The state created its own medical aid in 2005 called GEMS. The Government Employees Medical Scheme was registered on January 1, 2005, in accordance with the Medical Schemes Act 131 of 1998. The scheme reports to the Registrar of the Council for Medical Schemes and is defined as a body corporate that undertakes liability related to its members' healthcare benefits in exchange for receiving contributions. GEMS is a separate legal entity that does not form part of any government department or public entity.

GEMS collect contributions from most public servants and the state, but what seems to puzzle is that it has services outsourced to the following private companies:

- ASI – telemarketing services
- Europ Assistance – Emergency Medical Evacuation Dispatch (EMED)
- DENIS – dental management services
- Healthi Choices –maternity programme; wellness screening services
- Medikredit – pharmaceutical benefit management services
- Medipost pharmacy – chronic medicine courier pharmacy
- Medscheme contributions and debt management services
- Medscheme Health Risk Solutions (MHRS) – managed care services
- Metropolitan Health – membership and claims services
- Metropolitan Health – correspondence services
- Opticlear – optometry management services
- Thebe Health Risk Management joint venture – HIV/AIDS disease management services
- Universal Healthcare Services – chronic medicine management services; strategic managed care services

There is a very big opportunity within GEMS to create employment by the state for some of those services. Despite its challenges, GEMS is better functioning than most state entities. The state could adopt the same method to have an insurance institution cater for its massive appetite. Alternatively, it could assist up and coming black companies to be at the forefront of such services, instead of crying foul every time about wealth not distributed equally in the country. The state can just be a shareholder with about 20% or 30% in those companies, enough to have voting rights but not to control the institutions.

This is just an observation and a lot of research can be done by the smart ones. Ponder the quotes below:

> *"Let us never forget that government is ourselves and not an alien power over us. The ultimate rulers of our democracy are not a President and senators and congressmen and government officials, but the voters of this country."*
> **—Franklin D. Roosevelt**

> *"Government, even in its best state, is but a necessary evil; in its worst state, an intolerable one."* **—Thomas Paine**

> *"No government ever voluntarily reduces itself in size. Government programs, once launched, never disappear. Actually, a government bureau is the nearest thing to eternal life we'll ever see on this earth!"* **—Ronald Reagan**

I conclude with the following two quotes from Chris Hani:

> *"The perks of a new government are not really appealing to me. Everybody would like to have a good job, a good salary... but for me that is not the be all of struggle. What is important is the continuation of the struggle... the real problems of the country are not whether one is in Cabinet ...but what we do for social upliftment of the working masses of our country."*

> *"What I fear is that the liberators emerge as elitists who drive around in Mercedes Benz's and use the resources of this country to live in palaces and to gather riches."*

6

BASIC HOUSEHOLD/ PERSONAL FINANCIAL MANAGEMENT FOR FINANCIAL FREEDOM

Please note this is not by any means cast in stone nor financial advice that must be followed as I'm not a qualified financial adviser. Should you need any financial advice please consult a qualified person, not a family member or friends including me. When your body is sick, you consult a doctor (traditional or medical); the same principle should apply with your finances, consult a professional.

We have all at some point in our life made bad financial choices. We grow up being told money is the root of all evil. In my opinion, poverty is the root of all evil. Knowing how to manage your finances gives you peace of mind and confidence. You look forward to a new day knowing that you are stable even though not rich. The love of money is the problem to some people. We must learn to appreciate money, so it can stay longer with us, otherwise it will immediately go back where it's appreciated, which is shop tills, banks and bills.

Let's embark on this journey together as we explore how we can try to uplift our finances.

Investopedia has detailed a simple 10 steps one can follow as guidance by Will Kenton. (www.investopedia.com)

What is Personal Finance?

Personal finance is a term that covers managing your money as well as saving and investing. It encompasses budgeting, banking, insurance, bonds, investments, retirement planning, and tax and estate planning. It often refers to the entire industry that provides financial services to individuals and households and advises them about financial and investment opportunities.

Personal Finance Explained

Personal finance is about meeting personal financial goals, whether it's having enough for short-term financial needs, planning for retirement, or saving for your child's tertiary education. It all depends on your income, expenses, living requirements, and individual goals and desires—and coming up with a plan to fulfil those needs within your financial constraints. But to make the most of your income and savings it's important to become financially literate, so you can distinguish between good and bad advice and make savvy decisions.

10 Personal Finance Strategies

The sooner you start financial planning the better, but it's never too late to create financial goals to give yourself and your family financial security and freedom. Here are some of the best practices and tips for personal finance:

1.   *Devise a Budget*

A budget is essential to living within your means and saving enough to meet your long-term goals. The 50/30/20 budgeting method offers a great framework. It breaks down like this:

- 50% of your take-home pay or net income (after taxes, that is) goes towards living essentials, such as rent/ bond, utilities, groceries, and transport.
- 30% is allocated to lifestyle expenses, such as dining out and shopping for clothes.
- 20% goes towards the future: paying down debt and saving both for retirement and for emergencies.

It's never been easier to manage money, thanks to a growing number of personal budgeting apps for smartphones that put day-to-day finances in the palm of your hand. Here are just two examples: YNAB, aka You Need a Budget, helps you track and adjust your spending so that you are in control of every rand you spend. Meanwhile, Mint budgeting app, streamlines cash flow, budgets, credit cards, bills, and investment tracking–all from one place. It automatically updates and categorises your financial data as info comes in, so you always know where you stand financially. The app will even dish out custom tips and advice.

I'm old school, so I still use a spreadsheet that I update monthly. And I fear intrusion from apps.

2. *Create an Emergency Fund*

It's important to 'pay yourself first"' to ensure money is set aside for unexpected expenses such as medical bills, a big car repair, rent/bond if you get laid off, and more. COVID-19 has exposed a lot of us on this aspect.

Between three and six months' worth of living expenses is the ideal safety net. Financial experts generally recommend putting away 20% of each paycheque every month (which of course, you've already budgeted for!). Once you've filled up your 'rainy day"' fund (for emergencies or sudden unemployment), don't stop. Continue funnelling the monthly 20% towards other financial goals such as a retirement fund.

3. *Limit Debt*

It sounds simple enough: To keep debt from getting out of hand, don't spend more than you earn. Of course, most people do have to borrow from time to time–and sometimes going into debt can be advantageous, if it leads to acquiring an asset. Taking out a bond to buy a house is one good example. But leasing can sometimes be more economical than buying outright, whether you're renting a property, leasing a car, or even getting a subscription to computer software.

4. *Use Credit Cards Wisely*

Credit cards can be major debt traps. But it's unrealistic not to own any in the modern world, and they have applications other than as a tool to buy things. Facilitating travel bookings and flights is much easier with a credit card.

Credit just needs to be managed correctly, which means the balance should ideally be paid off every month, or at least be kept at a credit utilisation rate minimum (that is, keep your account balances below 30% of your total available credit). Given the extraordinary rewards incentives on offer these days (such as cash back), it makes sense to charge as many purchases as possible. Still, avoid maxing out credit cards at all costs, and always pay bills on time. One of the fastest ways to ruin your credit score is to constantly pay bills late–or even worse, miss payments.

Remember that credit card money is easily accessible but it's not yours and you should never make a mistake of including it on your budget as extra income.

Using a debit card is another way to ensure you will not be paying for accumulated small purchases over an extended period–with interest.

5. *Monitor Your Credit Score*

Credit cards are the main vehicle through which your credit score is built and maintained, so watching credit spending goes hand in hand with monitoring your credit score. If you ever want to obtain a lease, mortgage bond, or any other type of financing, you'll need a solid credit history behind you. Factors that determine your score include how long you've had credit, your payment history, and your credit-to-debt ratio.

In South Africa, the following guidelines are followed:

- 650 to 999 is minimum risk
- 620 to 649 is low risk
- 600 to 619 is average risk
- 581 to 599 is high risk
- 1 to 580 is very high risk

To pay bills, set up direct debiting where possible (so you never miss a payment) and subscribe to reporting agencies that provide regular credit score updates. TransUnion offer this service at a fee but you will be informed when someone does a credit check without your permission. By monitoring your report, you will be able to detect and address mistakes or fraudulent activity. The National

Credit Regulator allows you to obtain free credit reports once a year from Experian and TransUnion. You can register on clearscore. co.za and obtain an update of your credit score monthly for free.

6.   *Consider Your Family*

To protect the assets in your estate and ensure that your wishes are followed when you die, be sure you make a will and – depending on your needs – possibly set up one or more trusts. You also need to look into insurance: car, home, life, disability and long-term health insurance. And be sure to periodically review your policy to make sure it meets your family's needs through life's major milestones.

Other critical documents include a living will and healthcare power of attorney. While not all these documents directly affect you, all of them can save your next-of-kin considerable time and expense when you fall ill or become otherwise incapacitated. Most black families don't believe in wills and this has resulted in serious drama and accusations when an act of nature takes place.

And while they're young, take the time to teach your children about the value of money and how to save, invest, and spend wisely. Kids must be taught all the basics of handling money and donating; they must be on your budget for their allowance. Open bank accounts for them so they can learn from an early age how to save and only use what they have.

7.   *Pay Off Student Loans*

There are a myriad of loan-repayment plans and payment reduction strategies available to graduates. If you're stuck with a high-interest rate, paying off the principal sum faster can make sense. On the other hand, minimising repayments (to interest only, for instance), can free up other income to invest elsewhere or to put into retirement savings while you're young and will get the maximum benefit from compound interest. Avoid all tempting small loans that are not needed while still having other loans to pay.

8.   *Plan (and Save) for Retirement*

Retirement may seem like a lifetime away, but it arrives much sooner than you'd expect. Experts suggest that most people will need about 80% of their current salary in retirement. The younger you start, the more you benefit from what advisors like to call the magic of compounding interest – how small amounts grow over time. Setting aside money now for your retirement not only allows it to grow over the long term, but it can also reduce your current income taxes if funds are placed in a tax-advantaged fund. Speak to a financial adviser to maximise all the benefits available. By not doing so, you're giving up free money!

9.   *Maximise Tax Breaks*

Due to an overly complex tax system, many individuals leave hundreds or even thousands of rands sitting on the table every year. By maximising your tax savings, you'll free up money that can be invested in the reduction of past debts, your enjoyment of the present and your plans for the future.

You need to start each year saving receipts and tracking expenditures for all possible tax deductions and tax credits. In short, a tax deduction reduces the amount of income you are taxed on, whereas a tax credit actually reduces the amount of tax you owe. Keep all medical receipts for all cash payments you made, where your medical aid could not cover you to obtain medical tax credits.

10. *Give Yourself a Break*

Budgeting and planning can seem full of deprivation. Make sure you reward yourself now and then. Whether it's a vacation or an occasional night on the town, you need to enjoy the fruits of your labour. Doing so gives you a taste of the financial independence you're working so hard for. Just don't overdo it by trying to keep up with Joneses. (*Keeping up with the Joneses* is an idiom referring to the comparison to one's neighbour as a benchmark for social class or the accumulation of material goods).

• How to Spot an Investment Scam

A detailed article by Sue Torr was published on moneyweb.co.za.

I believe it can assist a lot to ensure that you stay alert and not fall victim and lose your hard-earned money. Despite heightened consumer awareness and education, more and more people fall prey to investment scams and fraud, especially in times of financial desperation. Increased access to technology, coupled with advances in artificial intelligence, means that investment scams are becoming more sophisticated, more cleverly disguised, and more difficult to identify. As a potential investor, there are steps you can take to verify any potential investment before parting with your hard-earned money:

➢ **Returns:** Any investment that promises returns that are greater than what investment markets are able to generate should immediately sound alarm bells. If the investment promises to double or triple your money in a short period of time, this should be an immediate cause for concern and a clear signal to back off. Remember, no investment is without risk, so if you're being offered guaranteed returns at ridiculously high rates, something is not right.

➢ **Jargon:** The marketing jargon used by the investment company should also give you clues to its credibility. Fraudulent investments are notorious for including words such as 'exclusive offer', 'select', 'elite', 'limited offer' or 'opportunity of a lifetime' in their marketing material.

➢ **Licensed:** The investment company should be licensed with the Financial Services Conduct Authority (FSCA) and should display their financial service provider number on all their marketing material, including their website, business cards, brochures and social media pages. If you're unsure, phone the FSCA and verify the organisation.

➢ **Bank account:** If the bank account of the investment is held in the name of a private individual, be suspicious. If it is a legitimate enterprise, it would hold a business account with a reputable financial institution.

➢ **Physical address:** The physical address of the organisation should also appear in all their marketing material, including websites and brochures – but don't take the printing of a physical address at face value. Use Google maps to look up the address and locate the actual building. Many legitimate companies pin their physical locations on Google maps as an added measure of credibility.

➢ **Free email accounts:** If you receive email communication from the investment company that is sent from any free email service such as Gmail, Yahoo or Hotmail, be very cautious. A legitimate investment company would operate off a secure email server and would not allow their customers' confidential information on free email servers.

- ➢ **WhatsApp:** Any investment opportunity that is communicated with you via WhatsApp should be regarded as circumspect, especially where the message was unsolicited. Besides being an inappropriate platform to conduct investment business on, it is also unprofessional and unsafe.

- ➢ **Private information:** Any unsolicited email, phone call or text message that invites you to participate in a scheme should raise red flags, especially if you are asked to provide private information. Specifically, any communication that requires you to input personal details, ID number, bank account details, SARS information, or to confirm anything via a hyperlink should be approached carefully.

- ➢ **Pay to play:** After piquing your interest with clever marketing jargon, many investment scams require you pay upfront fees to participate in the scheme, or to buy-in to the scheme. Any investment requiring that you 'pay to play' should be considered with suspicion.

- ➢ **Recruitment:** Many multi-level marketing schemes and Ponzi schemes operate a business model which requires each 'investor' to recruit more 'investors' in order to keep the scheme afloat. If the scheme involves any form of recruitment, it is likely to be some form of a pyramid scheme.

- ➢ **Lavish lifestyles:** Another ploy of investment fraudsters is running social media accounts that flaunt their lavish lifestyle with trips to exotic destinations, flashy cars and designer gear. Make a concerted effort to check on the Instagram, Facebook and Twitter accounts of both the individual you are liaising with and the company they represent.

- ➢ **Business model:** The company should take time to explain their business model to you, including underlying assets and how income will be generated. The business model should be wholly transparent and easy to understand. Investment scams are notorious for their complex business models and technical jargon. If you don't understand how your money will be used to generate investment returns, proceed with caution.

➤ **Google search:** Do a comprehensive search on Google using both the name of your contact person and the name of the investment company. This is an effective way of churning out any previous complaints or interactions that other people may have experienced. If your search reveals anything untoward, back away.

➤ **Giveaways:** Many investment scams offer free giveaways of goods and services in order to sweeten the deal. Giveaways can include bitcoin or other digital currency, holiday packages or free weight loss shakes. Reputable investment companies with good track records in the industry do not need to go to such lengths to attract investors, so this type of marketing should sound alarm bells.

➤ **Competitions:** If you receive communication that you qualify for a loan you didn't apply for or won a competition you didn't enter, take a considered approach. Your chances of winning the lottery are slim, especially if you didn't buy a ticket.

➤ **Pressure:** A reputable investment company will not pressure you into making a quick investment decision or convince you to invest more money. If you're being pressured into making a decision because the offer is limited or the offer is only available for a certain period of time, you should ask questions about its authenticity.

➤ **Track record:** Ask key questions about the company's track record. What is the company's reputation? Who owns the business? What are the directors' qualifications and experience? Does the business have any professional affiliations and/or outsourced partners? Ask for client testimonials, insist on a site visit and, if possible, ask an independent financial advisor for an opinion before parting with your money.

Further observations:

The majority of South Africans are heavily in debt, and the diagnosis is not that easy. Most honest people can attest that some of their debts are unnecessary and very painful to repay. Being blacklisted is never a wonderful thing. Just because the banks say your affordability is fine, does not mean you can truly afford things. The average debt to income in South Africa is estimated at 72,80%. This means you are only left with 27,2% to do your budget after debt.

I'm voicing the debt matter so I can highlight some of the dirty mindsets that made debt so easy. Most black people have an account of some sort with retailers, be it clothing, furniture, and yes even food, or a credit card, not to mention loans, overdraft and something called revolving credit. Don't be shocked; you can actually add some that I forgot. All of these are easily accessible to the point that they phone you to offer more credit without vetting your affordability appropriately. Actually, even if you were vetted correctly, that 'affordability' will still reduce what used to be your available take home income. Now if debt to income ratio is approximately 70%, this simply means that whatever you earn, you pay 70% of to debt, leaving you with 30%. So, when you increase the number of debts, you only have 30% to do that. Which leaves you with nothing. When you buy a car, they don't tell you what comes with such debt. Insurance, maintenance, petrol, a tracker and more problems. You will pose for a ribboned photo of the newly acquired car and a social media picture with some nice words, then reality strikes after a few months.

The creation of all these debts has led the black mind to be frustrated with a lot of things, as some of them were not needed. Can our minds comprehend the difference between a need and a want? I doubt it. But why have a clothing account for branded clothes? Why have an account for food? Why have an account for a full DSTV package when you spend 80% of your time not watching all those channels? What makes us glorify things that don't matter and leave important things out? We cannot take a loan to invest in a business or invest in ourselves by learning new skills, but we can take a loan for a funeral or Dubai holiday just for a hashtag 'I'm living the life'.

We know now why depression, something black people where never accustomed to, is real. It's the lifestyle we live. While there are people suffering genetically from depression, some have inflicted the illness upon themselves? I'm still generalising, don't forget that.

We fail our kids badly by not investing for or investing in them for that matter. We don't even invest in ourselves to upgrade our knowledge and skills yet we complain that we are not paid enough. We keep friends who don't inspire us, build us or encourage us to use our best abilities but expect to make it in life with a healthy bank balance. How many can look into their bank balance and smile in comfort? We instead smile in sad laughter because we know that we have done an injustice to our income.

We need to be conscience of how we do things and always remember it's easy to get into debt but it's never that easy to get out. Most debts are acquired satisfying wants that we actually can do without. A lavish birthday party for children financed by debt is the same as stealing from your future joy. The worst is you can acquire small debts from friends and ultimately not be able to repay them or repay them small amounts, which makes them angry. This might end good friendships. If you want a lavish lifestyle, make sure you can afford it, don't make it a burden for other people.

Any freedom is not easily attainable and financial freedom is just as difficult. It is easy to mess up and show off but you will be alone in the mess. You can be the go-to person for family and friends but when reality strikes and you are broke, you will turn into a philosopher in an instant. You will utter things like 'when days are dark friends are few', or new year resolutions to block and cut people who don't add value to your life. Meanwhile, you were the source of your own destiny and problems but never good at admitting it.

Last but not least, don't forget to delegate when needed. Even though you might be competent enough to do your own taxes or manage a portfolio of individual stocks, it doesn't mean you should. Setting up an account at a brokerage, spending a few rands on a certified public accountant (CPA) or a financial planner at least once–might be a good way to jump-start your planning. Only self-medicate your mind to do the right thing, then consult for the rest because you failed already when you lived beyond your means.

> *"Too many people spend money they earned. To buy things they don't want. To impress people that they don't like."*
> **—Will Rogers**

> *"An investment in knowledge pays the best interest."*
> **—Benjamin Franklin**

All men make mistakes, but a good man yields when he knows his course is wrong and repairs the evil. The only crime is pride." —**Sophocles**

"Pride goeth before destruction, and a haughty spirit before a fall." —**KJV, Proverbs 16:18**

7

GENDER-BASED VIOLENCE

What is Gender-Based Violence (GBV)? I will not attempt to explain it with my words but with what is already written the world over. I have only limited the literature to a few documents and articles I have read thus far and there is more literature on the topic for anyone to peruse.

I have chosen to write on this topic due to the past, current and possible future experiences I had. As I'm writing this in 2020, there is a huge increase in GBV due to lockdown restrictions in an attempt to curb the curve of COVID-19. In my opinion, GBV has always been huge and in front of us but now with the help of technology the speed of awareness is greater, but the help to our women and children is still a cry in the deep holes of hell.

At the rate we're going as human beings, something needs to be done. A lot of women are crying, saying men must do something, while men are also damaged and don't have a clue what to do. The bottom line is that men must stop the abuse, killing and discrimination. I have no idea but I will definitely write and raise my opinions. They are going to be wrong to some and right to many as there is no one size fits all. I will also generalise a lot with some factual research including my view and personal experience. To all who I will offend, I apologise in advance. The aim I have in my heart is to raise awareness and hopefully help to change the mindset to look at things differently.

• Brief International Literature on GBV

Gender-based violence is violence directed against a person because of their gender. Both women and men experience gender-based violence but the majority of victims are women and girls. GBV is a phenomenon deeply rooted in gender inequality and continues to be one of the most notable human rights violations within all societies. (*European Institute for Gender Equality*)

Intimate partner/family-related homicide is one form of interpersonal homicide that affects every country, irrespective of affluence and level of development. It is more evenly distributed across regions than other types of homicides that mostly affect males and is, on average, remarkably stable at the global level. In homicides related to intimate partners or family members, the relationship between victim and perpetrator is characterised by an emotional attachment, as well as other links, often of an economic or legal nature, whereas the perpetrator and victim in other types of homicide may or may not know each other. Two thirds of the victims globally are female and one third are male. (United Nations Office on Drugs and Crime)

In 18 countries (mostly in Europe), almost equal shares of victims are respectively killed by intimate partners (53%) and by other family members (47%). Though, in cases of victims killed by their intimate partners, 79 % per cent of victims are women, thus indicating that lethal violence within intimate relationships affects mostly women as victims. In absolute terms, the highest number of women who were killed by their partners or family members was found in Asia (19,700 women) and Africa (13,400 women). (United Nations Office on Drugs and Crime)

- ## **South African Literature and Content**

In South Africa, GBV falls under the Social Development Department. The following contact details for reporting abuse are listed on the GBV website:

➤ EMERGENCY CALL NOW LINE: 0800 428 428

➤ PLEASE CALL ME: *120*7867#, Supported by USSD

➤ Skype address: Helpme GBV for members of deaf community

➤ SMS 'help' to 31531 for persons with disability

I have never tried to use the above numbers to test their efficiency and effectiveness. I understand that there is a lot of frustration with our government currently, however, information is better than lack of it.

Let us look first into the different types of GBV as detailed on safespace (www.safespace.org.za):

Violence Against Women and Girls (VAWG)

GBV is disproportionately directed against women and girls. For this reason, you may find that some definitions use GBV and VAWG interchangeably.

Violence Against LGBTI People

However, it is possible for people of all genders to be subjected to GBV. For example, GBV is often experienced by people who are seen as not conforming to their assigned gender roles, such as lesbian, gay, bisexual, transgender and/or intersex people.

Intimate Partner Violence (IPV)

IPV is the most common form of GBV and includes physical, sexual, and emotional abuse and controlling behaviours by a current or former intimate partner or spouse and can occur in heterosexual or same-sex couples.

Domestic Violence (DV)

Domestic violence refers to violence which is carried out by partners or family members. As such, DV can include IPV, but also encompasses violence against children or other family members.

Sexual Violence (SV)

Sexual violence is "any sexual act, attempt to obtain a sexual act, unwanted sexual comments or advances, or acts to traffic, or otherwise directed, against a person's sexuality using coercion, by any person regardless of their relationship to the victim, in any setting, including but not limited to home and work." The European Institute for Gender Equality simplified it by stating that it is: any sexual act performed on an individual without their consent. Sexual violence can take the form of rape or sexual assault.

Indirect (structural) Violence

Structural violence is "where violence is built into structures, appearing as unequal power relations and, consequently, as unequal opportunities. Structural violence exists when certain groups, classes, genders or nationalities have privileged access to goods, resources and opportunities over others, and when this unequal advantage is built into the social, political and economic systems that govern their lives." Because of the ways in which this violence is built into systems, political and social change is needed over time to identify and address structural violence.

In addition, GBV can be physical, sexual, emotional, financial or structural, and can be perpetrated by intimate partners, acquaintances, strangers and institutions. Most acts of interpersonal gender-based violence are committed by men against women, and the man perpetrating the violence is often known by the woman, such as a partner or family member.

The following definitions are from the European Institute for Gender Equality:

Physical Violence

Any act which causes physical harm as a result of unlawful force. Physical violence can take the form of, among others, serious and minor assault, deprivation of liberty and manslaughter.

Psychological Violence

Any act which causes psychological harm to an individual. Psychological violence can take the form of, for example, coercion, defamation, verbal insult or harassment.

Economic Violence

Any act or behaviour which causes harm to an individual. Economic violence can take the form of, for example, property damage, restricting access to financial resources, education or labour market, or not complying with economic responsibilities, such as alimony.

I have chosen to exclude the statics recorded to date as we know how sensitive and real this topic is. This is human life I'm writing on, families, friends, children, communities and the country are affected and equally guilty as they are responsible to urgently come up with solutions. The state cannot fight this alone.

• **The Role of Families in the Fight Against GBV**

How many times have we heard this statement: "When I grew up, family was the centre ... in communities, my child was your child and vice versa ... the community took responsibility for the growth and protection of the child?" The truth is that for a person my age (early 40s), I have never witnessed the fullness of such. That is just my observation, and some people have experienced that, depending on the environment and background in which they were raised.

In the bible, 2 Samuel 13, we read of a story of Amnon and Tamar. Amnon was the son of David, and Tamar the sister of Absalom the son of David as well, making Tamar the half-sister of Amnon. Amnon loved or should I say lusted after his half-sister Tamar (a virgin) till he devised a plan to rape her. He succeeded and Absalom didn't take that kindly. He devised a plan and killed Amnon his half-brother. The law prevents us from taking matters into our own hands, however, the story was written many years ago, but to this day these things are still happening in our families.

As I said before, yes, I can generalise. The first point of resolving GBV should be families. Why am I saying this? Families are places where we start learning, where we are fed, and where kids learn from observation. Our cultural background is instilled from the family set up.

All families are different, and South African families, in particular black families have a single parent family set up or grandparents set up. If you are fortunate and grew up in a fully functional family with both parents consider yourself blessed. That doesn't mean fully functional families didn't have their own challenges like absent fathers, heavy-drinking parent/s and abusive parents. Others grew up in more than fully functional families which included extended family members with cousins and aunts or uncles under one roof. These are the realities of life in South Africa.

We grew up in families where we witnessed our mothers being beaten by our fathers; aunts beaten by uncles. Such fights would happen in front of children's eyes with no help. A child who would be brave enough to intervene and stop their father from beating their mother would be slapped and beaten so hard that they would never ever try again. Cursing and words unimaginable would be uttered near children. The worst was for mothers to wake up, make food for the same man who beat her to a pulp as if nothing was wrong. Words like, *ditaba tsa batho ba babedi ha di kenwe* (love affairs are between two people and no one must intervene) were normal. To expect normality from kids growing up in such an environment defeats logic but is never an excuse.

Philandering fathers have a sense of entitlement to their wife's body. When things didn't go their way, they resorted to beating the mothers and kids. When questioned about their behaviour they would remind the mothers that a man must not be asked questions. It would be a joke around male friends that *monna ke selepe* (a man is an axe, he can be borrowed). Concepts like *nyatsi e tiisa motse* (the other woman helps to build the family) are common. But when the same fathers experienced trouble in their extended relationship/family, they would come home and extend the anger to people who had nothing to do with it. Fathers who thought it was normal not to come back home on pay day or for the whole weekend, when questioned, would lash out. Such things are still happening and perpetrated by our peers, who think they are macho by showing their power over women.

Rape was the norm when I was growing up but it was something we heard from the streets only. The reality is that rape happened even within the family. Fathers have forced themselves on their own daughters or commented in a manner that will cause any sane person to cringe. Uncles have raped their nieces, brothers have committed incest with their sisters and cousins. All of these things happened inside the family set-ups and are still happening to this day and swept under the carpet. Mothers have been known to keep such things under wraps as they have been victimised and raped themselves by the same culprits. Other mothers told their daughters not to speak about this as it would break the family and they had nowhere to go as they were dependent on the father (animal) who was the perpetrator.

Family meetings and relatives don't do much to assist the fight against GBV. When a daughter is getting married in most African cultures, she is put with elderly women and given advice (*ukulayiwa*) by the same damaged old women. The most common advice will be 'a man is the head of the family and must be respected, give him your whole body even if you are tired, make him food and clean for him.' To my disgust there are even songs to such effect rubber stamping the slavery of women. Songs like *monna ga a batliwe payslip* (don't ever ask a man about his payslip), *umakoti ungowethu, uzosiphekela asi ayinele* (the bride is now ours, she will cook and clean for us) are sung joyously. Religions rubber stamp the same sentiments. They proclaim 'it's our culture'. What kind of culture condones rape, abuse and slavery?

The man, on the other hand, is told that he must take care of his family and religion will add, love your wives, and wives respect your man. The same religion has orders like slaves obey your earthly masters with deep respect and fear. One wonders then where love is when women bear all the pain. The advice given to a man, ultimately gives him power over the woman, while the woman's wellbeing and existence is removed completely.

Mothers of daughters will advise their daughters not to embarrass them by returning from their marital homes when things get tough. Family and parents will utter disgusting words if the married woman can't bear children, giving the man an unvoiced right to go philander and have children with other women. Effectively they are not giving the poor woman a chance to run back home where there was a bit of warmth and safety.

We have fathers who have never taken their daughters out for a date and teach their daughters how to be treated. The same daughters will have daddy issues when they grow up to substitute the space of love they never felt from their fathers. Mothers are guilty of not teaching their boy child to respect women, nor to cook, clean and take care of himself. All this is a pipe dream because they failed dismally to ensure that future generations are well-groomed adults. All this is happening under the watchful eyes of families.

Young boys and girls become teenagers despite a damaged past and go out into the world to confront the joy or pain that comes. They start relationships but carry a broken spirit. Young women have never had a platform to talk about the rape and abuse they experienced. They continue to start a family yet their soul is full of hate and disgust at men. The man only knows the woman to be a shouting machine, and in his anger retaliates with what he saw his father or uncle do as if it's a normal thing, just to silence the voice of the woman who is crying to be heard.

Families are guilty of not protecting their children, guilty of not protecting other daughters who marry into that family, while knowing that their son is evil, disrespectful and beats anyone who walks or disagrees with him. When the poor woman reports him, they ask the woman what she did. What have we become as human beings to let go of Ubuntu and loving our children? What happened to the child of the community?

Poverty within families and GBV have contributed to a point where many are trapped because the economy and lack of support from relatives is non-existent. Women find themselves with their kids trapped, living with an animal that is supposed to love and care for them. Just because he paid *lobola* (dowry) he feels entitled to owning that person.

It is very difficult to find a woman right now with no history or knowledge of abuse. Consider yourself lucky if you have never witnessed such or experienced such. Speak out for a family member and stand up for their rights. A lot of women right now hate their fathers for the abuse they experienced or witnessed and some hate their mothers for their silence and failure to defend them or ill words they uttered to them. Kids deserves to be respected and to grow up in a safe environment. Families are the backbone and the start for such safety.

Jim Carrey said on marriage, "Whoever created marriage was creepy as hell. Like I love you so much I'm going to get the government involved so you can't leave."

• The Role of Society in the Fight Against GBV

Gendered power inequality rooted in patriarchy is the primary driver of GBV. GBV is more prevalent in societies where there is a culture of violence, and where male superiority is treated as the norm. A belief in male superiority can manifest in men feeling entitled to sex with women, strict reinforcement of gender roles and hierarchy (and punishment of transgressions), women having low social value and power, and associating masculinity with control of women.

These factors interact with a number of drivers, such as social norms (which may be cultural or religious), low levels of women's empowerment, lack of social support, socio-economic inequality, and substance abuse. In many cultures, men's violence against women is considered acceptable within certain settings or situations – this social acceptability of violence makes it particularly challenging to address GBV effectively.

In South Africa, GBV "pervades the political, economic and social structures of society and is driven by strongly patriarchal social norms and complex and intersectional power inequalities, including those of gender, race, class and sexuality." (Safespace.org.za)

The society we grew up with had taught us that raped women were damaged. A raped woman is guilty, and questions like 'what she was wearing? what she did? why she went there? what she was doing with boys? 'follow the incident'. Accusations such as 'she likes men' (*sy is jags*), 'she flirts too much', 'she is too beautiful', 'she is too proud', 'she thinks she is clever', 'she deserved it' and all other rubbish is thrown at a wonderful young or old woman. When a woman is over 30 years old and unmarried she is   called a *lefetwa* (basically she must forget about marriage as she is old) and when she has no children she is subjected to nonsense names. Some are dished out by women themselves to bring each other down, not understanding their situation. Who said having children is the ultimate achievement to be classified as a woman, a caring parent, a loving person? This is a one-dimensional diagnosis dished to a woman, when it might be the man with a low sperm count who cannot produce children. Such is the wicked society with factory faults we live in.

Our society has lost its values of community building; they have become socialites. The society that says they mind their own business are the same people who gossip behind closed doors at the demise of other children. Jealousy has ruined good human beings to the extent that they wish evil on others. This is a society that knows abusers and yet keeps quiet. Kids and women are killed daily by known relatives or neighbours who are being protected by their families. We are riddled by a society that ignores a girl child's pregnancy, a teenager who is stressed out and screams when she takes the child and throws her in a pit toilet or aborts the pregnancy.

Our society is so guilty of keeping quiet and saying that they mind their own business. We are guilty of not defending the weak and poor. We are guilty of accommodating and befriending such animals who rape and abuse women and children. We are guilty of treating the LGBTI people with hate, disgust and exerting punishment; raping or killing them just because of their different sexual preferences. Why must it take death for a society to cry, why must it take death for a society to react, why must it take death for people to speak words like, we saw it would end in death? If God is listening to the prayers of society, then Heaven is not for our society.

When a woman returns from her marriage, the same society will be judging her as a failure. Comments like 'she couldn't keep a man, what makes you think she will listen to anyone?' label her. When she was crying that the man beat and ill-treated her, the same society said 'hold on and be strong'. How much strength can one have in life? When a man is abused, the same society says 'he is bewitched', 'he needs a prophet or a strong sangoma to vomit the *korobela* (muthi/ love portion)'. But what puzzles me is that the same diagnosis never applies when a woman is in the chains of a bad or abusive relationship. How double standards are applied between genders puzzles me.

The role of the society is huge when it is effective. We can ensure that there is safety for every child and woman. We can ensure that social media and all platforms available are utilised to the maximum to prevent any further abuses and killings. As a society, we have no right to judge, talk about things we don't know or even analyse anyone. Our duty is to support and be there without trying to make anyone inferior. Mistakes will always happen. Bad choices will always happen, but no one must pay with their lives, no one must be raped or abused. It is worse to face physical and emotional abuse, and then come to face financial abuse at home. These are the realities faced by a whole lot of women in our country and it's disgusting to say the least.

• The Role of the Government and Law in the Fight Against GBV

The information below has been documented under literature, but I have decided to detail it as it appears on gbv.org.za with additional information. The aim is to quote what the government and law say. The opinions and observations of the practicality of these laws follow.

USEFUL NUMBERS TO KEEP	
SAPS Emergency Services:	10111
Childline South Africa	Report child abuse to Childline South Africa's toll-free line: 0800 055 555.
GBV Command Centre	Contact the 24-hour Gender Based Violence Command Centre toll-free number 0800 428 428 to report abuse
South African Police Service	Report all cases of rape, sexual assault or any form of violence to a local police station or call the toll-free Crime Stop number: 086 00 10111.
Legal Aid South Africa	Call the toll-free Legal Aid Advice Line 0800 110 110 for free legal aid if you who cannot afford one.
Commission for Gender Equality	Report Gender Discrimination and Abuse: 0800 007 709
South African Human Rights Commission	Call 011 877 3600 to lodge a complaint about human rights violations.
Domestic violence Helpline:	Stop Women Abuse: 0800 150 150
AIDS Helpline	0800 012 322

- ## **What to do if you or someone else is being abused?**

➢ Provide the necessary help and support to a friend, family member or someone else who has experienced or is experiencing GBV.

➢ Do not suffer in silence: If you are being physically, psychologically (mentally), emotionally or sexually abused, talk to someone you can trust such as a friend, neighbour, relative, spiritual leader or elder, doctor or counsellor.

➢ Get professional help by:

  - pening a criminal case against the abuser for rape, sexual assault or physical violence.

  - Applying for a Protection Order at your nearest Magistrate's Court.

- ## **What is a Protection Order?**

It is a written order that is issued by a magistrate to stop any person from committing any act of domestic violence against another person with whom he or she has a domestic relationship.

➢ The person who seeks the Protection Order is referred to as the complainant while the person who has or allegedly committed an act of domestic violence and against whom the Protection Order is applied is called the respondent.

➢ The complainant of domestic violence must be or must have been involved in a domestic relationship with the respondent to qualify for a Protection Order. In terms of the Domestic Violence Act of 1998 (as amended), a domestic relationship means a relationship between a complainant and a respondent if they:

- Are or were married to each other in terms of any law, custom or religion.

- Are of the same or opposite sex, live or have lived together in a marriage or single relationship.

- Are the parents of a child or are persons who have or had parental responsibility for that child.

- Are family members related by blood relation, affinity or adoption.

- Are or were engaged, dating or in a customary relationship.

- Share or recently shared the same residence.

- **Persons who can apply for a Protection Order:**

  - The victim of domestic violence;

  - Any minor without the assistance of a parent, guardian or any other person; Any person on behalf of the minor without the assistance of the minor's parent, guardian or any other person;

  - Any person on behalf of the complainant who has a material interest in the well-being of the complaint including counsellors, health workers, police officers, social workers or teachers. The written consent of the complainant is required, unless the complainant is a minor, mentally retarded, unconscious or is found by the court to be unable to give such consent.

The respondent will only be arrested upon breach of the terms of the order by failing to comply with the terms, such as persisting with the physical or verbal abuse.

Commitment of SAPS to victims of domestic violence

It is the commitment of the SAPS to treat victims of domestic violence with sensitivity and care. As police officials:

➢ we will treat victims with respect and protect your dignity;

➢ listen to what victims have to say;

➢ not insult or blame or suggest that it was their own fault that they were abused;

➢ assist you with empathy and care;

➢ inform victims of their rights and options.

To ensure that this has been done:

➢ we will ask victims to sign the Occurrence Book at the police station;

➢ provide victims with a notice in a language they understand, and explain how they should proceed;

➢ make an effort to find someone to speak to the victim in the language he/she understands;

➢ take a victim's statement in privacy and not in the presence of the abuser or the public;

➢ decide on the basis of your statement, whether to arrest the abuser and take his/her firearm, as well as determine the victim's needs and how to assist him/her;

➢ serve a protection order on the person against whom it was made, as directed by the court;

➢ keep a copy of the protection order and record every arrest made as proof for victims;

➢ note your complaint in the Incident Register at the station as further proof that you reported the matter.

Is all the above information helpful in practice?

I have never reported a GBV crime and am as guilty as our society for the deafening silence or ignorance. I however have spoken to a few survivors, victims or affected women hence I'm writing this information down. Our police have been criticised a lot, so too the government and justice system. We have seen how some cases go to court and have been left perplexed at the sentences. The cry of the majority of citizens is that the death penalty should be reinstated to deter such crimes especially where there is sufficient indisputable evidence of the crime.

The Protection Order has never assisted anyone because by the time the police react, if they ever do, the perpetrator has already committed the crime, killed children and their mother. Children are being raped and one wonders what kind of animals we are living with who get aroused by children. What kind of robbery is it that ends in rape and murder? The truth is that such things are happening while we have the law, police and justice system that is supposed to protect everyone.

A woman walks into the police station to report a crime or abuse only to find the man is well-known by the same police. The woman is advised to resolve this matter with her partner 'as adults'. At times, the police say some people have relationships that are coming to an end, but the woman is unhappy with that, then reports abuse only to find out there is no abuse. The role of the police is to take action and uphold the law with no fear or favour but the current reality is that such is not being done effectively. Policemen and women must be effectively trained to handle GBV; their speed of response and reaction should be lightning fast.

The justice system is evidence-based, but loss of life, abuse, molestation, mutilation go unpunished time and gain due to the state's weak case despite the defence having full knowledge of what happened. How does one sleep at night? And there are laws governing certain professions to ensure client confidentiality is kept as such. My question is, if you are a lawyer, and you represent a rapist, killer or child molester, where is your moral obligation? Where do you draw the line? Is money the driver or ego of wanting to be the best and most-feared lawyer? I will never understand it but do not judge anyone for their profession.

The justice system that brings these animals back to society and says it's because they served a jail term and rehabilitated. That same criminal commits rape and murder again. Do we need to review the system? I say yes.

During 2010 Soccer World Cup in South Africa, there were 56 special courts established country wide at a cost of around R45 million. The speed of prosecution ranged from 24 hours to a few days. Our government failed to capitalise on that system after the world cup, when they could have done that for all valid small crimes, so that our high courts could dedicate time to real issues such as GBV at a faster speed and accuracy.

Our government should ensure there are more safe houses for women and children in desperate need of domestic violence. Most women have no way out, due to being rejected by families, relatives or have no one/ nowhere to go to. It is not enough that there are helplines and protection orders. Some men are providers for their families yet they are not wonderful human beings. The fact that a woman drops a case or refuses to open one shouldn't be a deterrent to dealing decisively with the culprit. Provide help and a kick start to life to the affected away from the abuser. Why must the reaction come when there is death? Mental health evaluation and assistance should be highly prioritised by the state. Abused women have suffered from emotional abuse, which has taken their confidence and self-worth, long before it gets physical. Most will be rejected by families because she told them she loved him, despite deep rooted real fears.

• The Role of Men in the Fight Against GBV

President Ramaphosa, while he was still deputy president said, in July 2017, "Each one of us, regardless of our upbringing or social circumstances, has been given the power of free will. We can make a decision, each of us, not to engage in violence, not to perpetrate abuse. We are responsible for our actions."

Anna Ford said, "It is men who face the biggest problems in the future, adjusting to their new and complicated role."

Vaclav Havel added, "The real test of a man is not how well he plays the role he invented for himself, but how well he plays the role that destiny assigned to him."

Not all men are bad, I agree, but...

The world has evolved and changed a lot yet the mindset of too many men is still stuck in the dark ages. Men still think they rule over women and have power over women. They use their masculinity to overpower women because that's the only thing available to them. Yes, I am generalising, and if the shoe fits, wear it. Who came with the damning quote or law or rule that a man is the head? If you say to me it's God, then does God say man must rape, abuse, kill women? I refuse to accept things that don't make sense. Man is born of a woman, a process that takes about nine months. Yet man, to this day, disrespects women, although they respect their mothers and sisters to some extent but never a woman they desire or form a relationship with.

The time has come that man must stop the silence and justification of nonsense. I have heard it all – 'You have paid for her school fees, you have supported her, you bought her a car and a house, you married her, you loved her, you are her soul mate, you are her ride or die, you are hashtag relationship goals, you made her, you found work for her, you gave her work, you are the baby daddy, she lied about the baby daddy, you caught her in bed with another man, she was only interested in your money'.

None of this justifies you as a man to kill her or beat her up. Every human being has a choice. If she chooses to leave you or hurt your heart, you are not a tree. Move, leave her in peace with a clear conscience and let karma deal with her, if there is such a thing. Most importantly as a man, take stock on how you can do things better next time. Don't carry on with the hate burden to the next relationship.

What kind of men are we that we look at a woman solely to sleep with her? When you are 'friend zoned' as they say, the stupid male ego gets tainted. Men are simply failing to be friends purely for fear of being classified as a cock blocker or called other wicked names by factory faulted males with egos that can inflate a parachute.

From the rush of male testosterone, men have classified themselves conquerors of women. They count how many women they have slept with and somehow become glorified as heroes, *isoka lamanyala, sejabana* (player). A true gentleman knows that a woman who is interested, will have signs to show you. And that doesn't mean an obvious win, as you will still have to work hard to prove yourself. Just because she gave you her number, thinking she likes you is utterly foolish.

The silence of man is embarrassing and what is worse is that we have such friends in our midst. Anthony Walters said, "Many guys are afraid to speak out, even if they see one of their friends whistling and calling women vulgar names as they pass. This is behaviour that cannot be tolerated, we should speak to our friends instead of simply laughing or playing along, as they humiliate women in this way."

We as men must face the truth that we are the cause of GBV. We are damaged and need help. Why do we have to resort to violence when things don't go our way? Just because you lose an argument or debate in the house does not justify slapping her or banging doors to instill fear in her. You are asked a simple question like why are you late or where did you sleep? You attempt to concoct a story that even a primary school child will not believe, and when she doesn't believe you, she is in the wrong and deserves to be *bliksemed* or *moerd* (beaten).

We have men with sick minds who get aroused by children in our midst. They go all out to rape and threaten the child not to speak or kill the poor child because they are known by the family and community. There are men who deprive their kids and women of economic benefits and yet act macho on the streets buying alcohol for everyone. They think that by paying alimony they are doing the baby mother a favour. When they have parted ways with the baby momma they still want to have control over who she is dating or seeing. Look deep within as a man, especially at all your abusive nature that when you father a baby girl and leave her, the woman will find love elsewhere and you better pray that man is not also a sick rapist, abuser or killer of your offspring.

Men cheat and lie a lot but cannot take it when it happens to them, yet we must believe as males we are strong. We are weak to the core and must admit to it and deal with our weakness, not take it out on women. A man who always suspects and controls his women knows what he is afraid of. Either he didn't heal from the past relationship, or he is a philandering man and thinks the woman does the same thing.

We have thugs around us who are not reported to the police because they are after money. Yet those same men hang around with other imbeciles who commit crimes to gain money and still rape women to finish off the job. What kind of a sick mindset is that? It clearly says then we must report all crimes and stop this silence. It is our business and duty to protect our sisters, daughters and mothers.

As men we need to understand that we don't own women. We don't control women. We don't rape women. We don't beat women. We don't abuse and kill women and children. The time is now that we make a noise. Let us own up to real problems. We have no skills whatsoever to deal with the 'new' man we must be in the new era. We must unlearn the old habits we saw in our fathers and learn to listen, understand and be calm. Social activism is not enough and does nothing to shake the current situation. Just because you can type hashtag, or comment on a social media page doesn't mean you support GBV. We need the legal system to change and be harsh in deterring violence.

A real man builds his woman, support his woman, grows his woman, doesn't fear that the woman makes more money than him, and doesn't get intimidated by her male friends. A real man loves unconditionally. He respects all women with no exception. He has female friends and doesn't expect favours from them. He supports other women with their personal problems without getting aroused. A real man knows how to cook, clean, iron and take care of himself. If he doesn't know how, he knows he can hire help and order take-aways easily. He also understands that a woman is not his slave.

A real man knows how to resolve his own relationship issues without involving his mom or the woman's parents. He knows that disagreements and differences of opinion exist in relationships and respects that. There is no need to utter painful words that cannot be reversed. He knows that he is his own person with dreams and goals and so is she. He has real friends and she has real friends and he does not dictate to her about her friends.

A real man knows that if the best he gave in a relationship is not good enough, he can walk away with a clear conscience and not be bitter. He knows he gave it his all. He will not punish his offspring because of the mistakes of his ex-woman. If he found a woman with a child and stayed long enough to play a father role to that child, he doesn't suddenly turn his back on that child because her mother did him harm. When he buys clothes for his biological children, he buys for the child he helped raise. A real man knows how to treat a woman, give money when you have, spoil her with gifts. A wise man knows the woman is right and apologises with a smile, hug and a kiss on the forehead, even when he is not wrong. This is the kind of a man the new world needs. This violence must end. Peace is always better than war.

I end this with a Julius Caesar quote: "Cowards die many times before their actual deaths."

• The Role of Women in the Fight Against GBV

Can women stop judging each other so harshly? Stop hating yourselves. Love yourselves. Stand for each other. Respect one another. Support one another. The world needs you and loves you.

An injury to one is an injury to all. Don't give up the fight. It's hard I know, and you don't deserve the treatment you receive from men.

You don't need to be defined by strength and pain anymore, you are human and deserve the right to be defined as yourself. Every time a black woman is celebrated, there must be some double effort she has endured, a pain hidden deep inside, the survival of a gruesome act by a man. Why? You walk around with fear yet you are more powerful than any known creature in this world. Men fear your strength and power; your knowledge and intelligence are beyond any education system. The world knows that if you are to rule, the world will have peace. Males don't want to let that happen. Please unite.

Stop being naïve and see the signs always. An abusive man will always show you signs. They can be verbal or otherwise but never think you are going to change him. Love with your heart but always take the brain with you. Listen to sound advice. When you are warned about him, be open minded and look for the truth. Don't say they are jealous and discard it. There is no smoke without fire. Interview your potential suitor, see if he meets your goals and ambitions. Don't just say he is cute and smells nice. Those things don't sustain a relationship.

Remember, GBV is also not limited to males, females commit it too. It can include simple things such as slapping him when you are having a heated argument; pushing him around when you are angry; smashing his phone against the wall or breaking his car windows; splashing water or a drink in his face when you are angry; uttering vulgar words to him or bringing him down by telling him he is useless; comparing him to other males when you know how hard he is trying; and denying him the right to see his child/ children because you are bitter about the relationship ending unceremoni-ously. There is no justification for such actions.

Please avoid at all costs or stop embarrassing the other woman who slept with your so-called man, blame your man, if anything. Beating another woman is undignified and unnecessary. You can't undo the act, neither will you teach anyone a lesson. Have pride and walk away.

If you want to be treated with respect in a relationship show respect. Heal before you take your past to a new relationship. No one must pay for the mistakes they didn't create. Hiding your past pains and revealing them in your anger is not going to help any relationship you go into. No one is a prophet or sangoma in a relationship who can foretell what might be troubling you, but communication can go a long way.

I know there are many bad women (termed *di tiki-line*) as well, who actually embarrass a whole lot of good, hardworking women, just as there are many man who are very bad (f boys). I'm more concerned about the ones who cry in vain, the ones who push yet are victims of discrimination, the ones who have lost hope yet need faith to leap. I'm celebrating women just for being women. You are not a single mom, you are not a survivor, you are not a victim, you are a woman and have a name. You are beautiful just the way you are. Be proud of that fact. God and nature didn't make mistakes by creating you.

I can never write anything about you, except that I apologise as a man for such violence.

I leave you with this quote from the female hustlers, "You attract what you think. Once you establish yourself as independent, people like you will come your way out of nowhere. And that's just the universe reminding you that when you see something beautiful in yourself, others can see it and admire it as well."

8

VOICES OF THE POWERLESS BUT POWERFUL... IMBOKODO (ROCK)

This chapter is dedicated to all women in the country. I have deliberately included the quotes below to inspire all women to believe they can do anything they set their minds to. I have requested all women I know within my circle to voice their thoughts, opinions, suggestions, criticisms or anything they think should be known, without being prejudiced. It can be on gender-based violence, the economy, life in general, discrimination, fears and hopes, empowerment, working together as women, male dominance, business and politics, etc. A chapter is not enough to capture what women have on their chests; they need a bigger platform.

> *"It's the fire in my eyes, And the flash of my teeth, the swing in my waist And the joy in my feet. I'm a woman Phenomenally. Phenomenal woman, That's me."*
> **—Maya Angelou**

> *"The fastest way to change society is to mobilise the women of the world."* **—Charles Malik**

> *"She stood in the storm and when the wind did not blow her way, she adjusted her sails."* **—Elizabeth Edwards**

"*A woman is the full circle. Within her is the power to create, nurture and transform.*" —**Diane Mariechild**

"*I am not free while any woman is unfree, even when her shackles are very different from my own.*" —**Audre Lorde**

"*Honour your daughters. They are honourable.*"
—**Malala Yousafzai**

"*Women of South Africa are some of the most powerful people on Earth. Change what you believe is possible for yourself.*"
—**Oprah**

"*A woman with a strong voice is, by definition, a strong woman.*" —**Melinda Gates**

"*To live my life to the fullest and experience each day as if it were my last, knowing that, nothing is impossible if you put your mind to it! To make a difference in the lives of those less fortunate than I am. To touch each soul that I encounter as I journey through life with compassion, dignity, humility and respect, in the full knowledge that irrespective of our circumstances we are all made in the image of God.*"
—**Dr. Thandi Ndlovu's life motto. (*Founder of Motheo Construction, MHSRIP)***

• The thoughts, opinions and suggestions from selected women I know:

Kanyi Tshisa commented on working together as women and GBV: *Women fail dismally when it comes to working together or even being unified under dire circumstances which require standing together. Often times we are exposed to the reality of women fighting against each other where there are chances of growth for one of them. They would rather have a man take up a leadership position than see another woman climbing the ladder – in any environment. Women need a lot of self-acceptance. We cannot deny that competition is healthy, but with women it goes a little further. It goes as far as backstabbing and deception, even if it means that it could possibly open doors for the rest. We still have a long way to go before we can fully achieve an image of women working together.*

GBV: This is an issue that requires a lot of attention. The number of cases reported increases exponentially with each year that goes by and they will continue to increase for as long as the perpetrators are being protected. Victims are always identified by name, age and where they stay but the perpetrators only by the title they withhold (i.e. boyfriend, husband, father etc). Our communities continue to protect these criminals and play blind to their actions for as long as the victims are not related to them. It is true that we will not understand until it happens to us – this too is a sad reality for GBV victims as they are not given the much-needed support to heal emotionally (if that's even possible). In most communities victims are made to feel deserving of such acts and often labelled by derogatory terms. We have a national register of sexual offenders but even this is not utilised to its full potential as it is not available to the public. If such information was availed to the public then women would be able to avoid getting into contact with these individuals because most GBV offenders are closely related to their victims.

We can also not ignore the fact that we have victims who protect their offenders, which makes it difficult for the community at large to intervene in any way. The law too, is limited to resolving such matters as victims refuse to take any legal actions.

Women live in fear. Trust gets knocked out of our senses with each case reported and sadly there is no running away from it because your offender could be living under the same roof with you, sharing meals with you and pronouncing their love for you every day.

Zama Mofokeng commented: *As a woman in South Africa I need a mask. A mask to shield me from racial injustice and to ensure that I get things according to merit and not the colour of my skin. This mask will heal my heart and soul when I see gruesome images of women and girls being killed every day in our country. It will ensure that I am not raped or killed today. I am scared, I fear for my children and their future. We have needed this mask for decades, however, it also needs to prevent me from playing the victim and stop the 'damsel in distress' behaviour.*

We need to fight, be strong and resilient. What legacy will I leave behind if today is indeed my last day?

I need to know that I have equipped those around me with the desire to be better. I need to know that in a world full of hatred, I often wore my heart on my sleeve. I loved and showed kindness even when my heart was breaking. We must clothe ourselves with love, kindness, forgiveness and all the so-called clichés. As women we need to have an eccentric resilience, often referred to as 'crazy' because nobody remembers normal. My mask is full of possibilities, what about yours?

Chrisie Adams on GBV: *Growing up, a young girl in my teens, I tried to find myself while experiencing dominance, corporal punishment/ discipline which left me and my siblings blue and black all over our bodies. As kids we were made to believe that this was lawful and necessary and* *assisted in grooming us for the life we needed to be ready for. One had to learn to cope with the demons this treatment caused inside of you while keeping 'die blink kant bo' because it would make a better person of you (though I beg to differ).*

Witnessing physical abuse to familiar women after the weekly end-of-work party, left scars deeper than you can imagine, which later in life would haunt you. Having been shouted at, embarrassed and belittled by a parent or elder just because they can, eventually robs you of your dignity, your confidence, the freedom to laugh spontaneously, too scared to even just smile. The verbal abuse which was always referred to as rubbish and non-existent was real, very real. What made it worse, the bystanders who just stood around watching, sometimes laughing but doing nothing to stop this insane behavior.

I believe, being a woman, we experience every kind of abuse in one way or another. It is caused by the hand of the gender who is supposed to guide us, protect us and uplift us. When the likes of a father, a brother, an uncle, nephew or close family friend turns into the nightmare you wish you could just awaken from, where can you hide? Where do you run to?

Times have changed or so we would like to think. Women became visible and independent workers while still being capable mothers, wives, teachers, nurses, you name it. Is this the cause behind the rage in men driving them to kill the backbone of our livelihood, our women?

As a child and teenager, being exposed to this left some deep layers of anger which I struggled with. There was no platform to help you fight against this injustice, there was nobody willing to listen or who thought it worthy enough to do something about it.

Where is the justice? Where is the law? Who protects our women and children?

Our Constitution provides for the right to life for every individual. Where is the right of all those women and children who are brutally murdered and raped by the hands of our men? Men blame us for their own brutal and selfish actions, trying to find justification for their weakness and loss of self-control. Some of them get arrested; serve a minimal sentence as punishment for taking another life thereafter they are just accepted back into society. Is this what we call justice? Where do you draw the line?

Our laws have failed us. Society has failed us. Our upbringing has failed us.

Gender based violence is not a new thing. It did not start yesterday or last month or last year or five years ago. It's been here way too long and nothing has been done about it for far too long. Even though they try to silence us, women are the driving force of our country. Without them, what will become of us?

What will become of our children? Where does it all end if we do not take a stand? God help us all.

> *"Each time a woman stands up for herself, without knowing it, possibly without claiming it, she stands up for all women."*
> **—Maya Angelou**

Gloria Moleleki wrote: *In this country (South Africa) do we only recognise physical or mental ability to have authority, to lead in strategic positions or is intellect gender based? Allow us women to be the change the world needs without fear of being prejudiced. We are born to bring life and bring with it the change in how the world perceives the relevance of this gender. Give us a chance to change, we might look powerless but inside we are powerful.*

In South Africa, we don't need to be muscular to have a legitimate right to walk peacefully in the streets, to enjoy shopping and entertainment, to go to work and to enjoy the peace and tranquillity of our homes without the fear, apprehension and insecurity which constantly diminish the quality and the enjoyment of lives.

Anastasia Samuels gave her opinions as follows: *Women in general are such fragile, sensitive beings and yet it's expected of us to maintain the household, take care of the kids, cater to her husband and maintain a full-time job to sustain their livelihood. Our challenge is that we tend to forget to focus on our own needs and this is where numerous difficulties creep in, like fatigue as a result of lack of sleep, weight gain or loss, decreased energy levels, to name a few.*

Contributing factors are for one, the expectation created of women to be submissive to men and being practised strictly in some cultures and religions. This practice led to a lot of suppression and non-equal opportunities. Proven statistics in the private sectors and even sports, reveal that men tend to earn more than women which is in most, if not all cases their peers, and what is sad is women have to work much harder than men to prove themselves. Handling all these responsibilities, women must stand strong and yet so fragile.

When a child gets hurt, they instantaneously call for their moms. Women are the anchors of their household. Working women tend to stress more when required to travel with work as their mind is working overtime to think of leaving dads or anyone outside her household in charge while she's gone. Women are such delicate beings and yet any form of abuse exists in all parts of life. Incidents of GBV have skyrocketed in our country and the world. It's sad how few perpetrators are being caught or prosecuted.

Our fragile elderly women and children especially are the targets of violence and deaths and should be protected and do not feel safe anywhere and a lot of the abuse and violence exists in their homes. The places where women are supposed to feel safe, but don't. Gone are the days of walking to shops, churches without being attacked. Are the lives of women worthless in today's society?

Another enemy is women having a lack of uplifting each other. Women would rather suppress or degrade one another to stand out. Women don't give compliments to each other to uplift confidence and pride in one another. Popularity contests are the order of the day and true friendships are very rare. Women carry their burdens privately and are too ashamed to share, in fear of being judged and belittled. What the world needs is unity and acceptance of each other and less criticism and rejection. Religion, culture, race and age should not matter. We all need acceptance and a sense of belonging. Leading by example and spontaneously giving a compliment means the world and everyone appreciates feeling a little special, even for just a little bit...

Adelaine Lewis added her view: *When I received the request to partake in this, my mind ventured into various directions and I found myself struggling to say what I think as I then realised I am probably one of the most outspoken and even opinionated, if you will, women I know. Some people take offence, and in my experience, it is for the most part, other women. I've often wondered why my counterparts found it so difficult to accept this characteristic and why they often misconstrued it with being cold and ruthless. Let me say this, I've learnt early on in my career in the public sector, that women, even those that we least expect it from, often use other women as stepping stones, to further their ambitions. I've also learnt that others compromise their own self-worth and respect to further their ambitions of obtaining higher earning positions. Hence, in a nutshell, mine, because I've witnessed and felt the backlash of it myself, speaks to the topic of women working together in the next paragraph.*

In my 20 plus years career working in government, I have often realised with great disappointment that there is only a small percentage of women who actually succeed in top management positions at a reasonably young age. This, despite the fact that we live in an era where strong women have fought for us to have equal rights and emancipation from male oppression. I said disappointed, because of this phenomenon of women 'selling' themselves has compromised the rest of us women employed, and those still striving to get to the top. My independently raised character cannot understand why women would be so willing to sacrifice their reputations and self-respect just to get ahead in the workplace.

On the other hand, I have empathy with the position so many of us find ourselves in, or know of someone who does, where you are forced to do just about anything to provide for yourself and your family. This being said, I am also not oblivious to the challenges that we as women face daily. Often, it is expected from us to be this superwoman who needs to attend to everyone else's needs. It ranges from a husband, children, extended family right up to your in-laws. And many a time, no help is offered in terms of how to live up to the expectation, it is left as a requirement which we cannot fail to deliver on. This concept, I believe, is bred from the culture that most black South African women, come from.

This next paragraph somehow speaks to my opinion on life in general, as I've experienced it, and, to a certain degree, also male dominance. I often reminisce on a saying that every coloured woman like myself has heard from our mothers. 'a woman's hand must be able do to anything' ('n vrou se hande moet vir niks verkeerd staan nie'). This saying was used frequently when we were groomed on cooking and keeping a good household so that we would be able to do so in our own homes one day. I suppose our beloved mothers felt they were preparing us for the future, and for many of us this lesson has been a useful one nonetheless. Yet, I also realised later on in life, that this was how we were conditioned to believe it is women's job to cook, clean, bear children and take care of a man. And this concept bred the idea that the man is superior in the house, irrespective of whether he actually deserves such a title or not.

I myself was left destitute by a man at a point when I needed him most and was left to play the part of mom and dad. In contrast, I have also been blessed to have known the other side, having a father worthy of respect and gratitude who did not demand respect, but earned it.

If I could, I would write an entire book on the complexities that face women today and how these complexities shape who we are. But, to other women out there struggling to find themselves, I say this, draw your strength from this scripture as I do, Philippians 4 v 13. "I can do all things through Christ who strengthens me." Life has taught me that all women, no matter where they come from, have been born with the inner strength to do anything and everything. It is all just a matter of tapping into it.

Kanyisile Maseko sent her thoughts: *Women can do anything they set their minds on: This is one thing women can do and excel in but society has always moulded the idea that no matter the idea, no matter what you do and achieve as woman, without the confirmation that man was involved, it is seen as null and void. Society needs to change the mindset and beliefs instilled in women that they can only be deemed as good enough if there is a male counterpart on her side. We have the strength to achieve anything we set our minds to; we also need to set our minds on the correct things to focus on. Give a woman R10, she can make you a meal – then come tell me we are incapable?*

Many things need to change in society. When a woman buys a five-bedroomed house, why must she be questioned that there is no one to fill it or that she must watch out she will scare men away. I say the men that will be scared are those not likely to be her counterpart if she's destined to have one. Success is measured by a woman's ability to marry, bear children and stay in that marriage no matter how tough or physical it may be. This is one of the things that needs to change. There is this saying that children are a gift from God; why then are women bashed when they cannot conceive in marriage? These are the type of things that drive unwanted behaviours in society, where desperate women feel the need for validation, go to extremes of kidnapping.

Women should learn that we are not responsible for changing and correcting the behaviour of men by being seen as the perfect partner who obeys everything. We need to learn that there is a thin line between being a partner and being a slave. Women must stop taking the bashing from society for being solely responsible for a divorce. You were married to someone else, not yourself. So why is it your failure alone? Black families need to stop turning their daughters away when they want to leave a marriage. You are kids and society.

Khanyisile Maseko added:

Money/Finance/Financial management: *Society blames women for loving money but it's the same society that teaches a girl child to choose a man wisely and choose a man that can provide for her from top to bottom. These are the things instilled in young women, that when they meet any guy, the primary purpose they think of is whether he can provide for me from top to bottom? And unfortunately, the rest of the characteristics are overlooked; hence we end up with abusive mentally ill men who think they own you because they are providing for you from top to bottom.*

We also should not be complacent as woman. Is it ok to really call your man to tell him there is no bread? Are we really that dependent and or programmed to look to the provider that we won't even go and buy bread even if we do have the money? As women, we need to be careful as well never to be disarmed indirectly when it comes to finance. Just because he makes the big bucks does not mean you should leave your Checkers cashier job. Maintain your financial independence; whatever he adds is a blessing, but never be disarmed financially because you may be opening yourself up to all sorts of dependence and abuse.

Being an individual in a relationship: *I have observed most of us women lose our individuality in relationships. Society has again taught us to be submissive and we take the submission to another level where we lose ourselves in the process. If you ask many women in serious relationships whether they are living the life they want they will tell you, No. Most will tell you, I wish I could go play golf on a Saturday afternoon but ubaba ka Sthe*

(Daddy of Sthe) wants xyz. My question is, when will you ever go play golf and have ubaba ka Sthe tag along? We leave it all to him to live his dream because we fear that we won't be seen as submissive, we won't be seen as supportive and engaged in the relationship.

Friends you keep: *As women we are competitive beings, whether it be in bigger bums, longer weaves etc. Our downfall is we never want to be like her, we want what she has, example, her husband can be the 'ideal' provider from top to bottom then you want her husband. Forgetting that the top to bottom providers also provide what they want to and where they see fit. The treatment she gets may not necessarily be the same you get simply because your ass is bigger.*

Sport: Stigma/ support: *Why is it that there are so few competitive black women sports professionals? Society again failing our young women because there's this certain age where you should be settled down and making babies. And your little 'hobby', no matter how excellent you are in it, has to take the back seat. I was very surprised to witness a once-vibrant lady in sport, who had to retire early because she got engaged and needed to spend more time at home with her husband and because she is now umakoti (bride) she can no longer wear anything above the knee. I nearly flipped. I thought, you are not even 30 and this is what the rest of your life will look like, Is it that difficult for society and black men to stand by their women when they pursue sport as a career? We are creating depressed, bitter individuals in the long run because what they live is not their lives but a life moulded by someone else.*

Carmen Reneke opined that: *Firstly, a woman needs to know her worth and purpose in this world. A woman will support everyone around her while her own heart is breaking inside and still remain strong and focused on what lies ahead. She can make herself heard in a group and can easily make life easier and pleasant for everyone close to her. The advantage of a powerful independent woman by a man's side is that she can be a threat* *if a man is weak or a motivation if a man is strong. In a relationship, she will be the one who will be picking up the pieces of a bad ass man who treated her like trash while there will be men looking from outside and wish they had her. If you find that woman who accepts you with all your mistakes and flaws, you should count yourself lucky.*

A woman is unfairly expected to understand a man's tormented soul while she is not the source of his misery. A woman will stay loyal, dedicated and determined to make a success of any relationship she enters into. My heart goes out to each and every woman in this cruel world, suffering at the hands of men hurting them emotionally and physically. Women need to support and stand up for each other, instead they judge one another so harshly. Men should be celebrating women for all they do and go through for them instead of abusing them. God made each and every woman unique in His eyes; we are His own original design. Women are the main caretakers of the family and they ensure that the family adjusts to the real life as well as challenges faced daily.

A woman is expected to always have a positive outlook on life and live every day to the fullest, despite all challenges and being called names. Empowerment of women will lead to a better country, improved economy since women can turn any small amount of money into gold. Women can turn a house into a home. Empowering women will ensure they act on their own authority without fear.

Tumi Hatla in her words said: *Occasionally I ask God, why was I born female...a black female at that? Don't get me wrong, I love myself and the woman I have grown up to be but damn God, my life would be slightly better if I was born a man. To get to this point it took years of constant self-reaffirmation, development and fellow females pouring into my life. And there are days when I don't believe it all.*

One of my first lessons as a young girl was around my safety. I was taught, constantly reminded and at times yelled at about being vigilant about the company I keep and my surroundings – where and when I walk and drive. If the sun set and I was not in the house, then my mother went into a mini panic mode. If I had to travel late alone then she would meet me at the taxi stop so I wouldn't walk alone after dark, even though I lived less than 300 metres from the taxi stop. The power and protectiveness of a mother...she would rather put herself in the line of danger than let me face the danger alone. When I was younger, I did not understand her logic but the older I got and the more senseless deaths I was exposed to, the more I understood where she was coming from. I still remember her walking me to the taxi stop in the morning and waiting for me at the same spot in the evening when I started working. I used to commute between Sebokeng and Johannesburg daily. A whole grown woman having an escort. I know without a shadow of doubt that she would not have worried if we lived in a society that loved, appreciated and protected their women...black women!

A simple jog alone around the block can potentially turn into me being a victim of rape, robbery and murder. Why? What did I do to not feel safe in my own environment? Feel unsafe in the company of any man – including my own blood? What irks me the most is that women are afraid of men who are born and raised by a woman. All human beings are born from a woman so why is it that the very same precious and important person is the most terrorised and vulnerable? How? But most importantly, why?

Why is it that our so called 'vulnerability' is used against us? This is not just from a safety perspective but in all aspects of life. For me to be noticed, I learnt the hard way that I needed to be twice or three times better than my black male counterpart but I needed to be 10 times better than my Caucasian counterpart (female or male). And that is what I have been doing for as long as I can remember. It is exhausting to be a strong black woman. Every time I step into the office, I must remind myself to put on my thick skin and take the punches with a smile. My work, and at times life, mantra is 'smile and wave' because if I didn't constantly remind myself to do so I would be in prison, unemployed or worse, dead. It is one thing to experience hardship from Caucasians, but it kills me to the core to experience all this from a fellow black man or woman.

Currently the world is hurting all because ALL WE DID WAS BE BORN BLACK. I am fuming, I am angry, I am hurting and if I am honest with myself, I am disheartened by it all. Can we stop having all these talks and protests; instead can we see the change we need? Can people – men, Caucasians, eintlik (actually) everyone at fault – just do the right thing every day? How is that we are still fighting the same issues and are experiencing the same threats as our great-grandparents, grandparents and parents?

From this disheartened heart I am expected to love – feel and give love. With what? From where? I am a firm believer in and of love and at the back of my mind I still have hope that I will find that special one whom I will spend the rest of my life with. But I won't lie, it's at the far back of mine. Largely because I have been hurt to my soul a few times. I loved and gave my all and it was not good enough. At some point I remember being told that I was scaring suitors because I have a few assets of my own that are typically acquired (or assisted) by men. Men are intimidated by a woman who has a lot of money... more than what they have. All this in 2020! I laugh at this because God knows I don't want a man who is intimidated by someone they don't know or are willing to get to know. I find this a paradox of a strong black woman's life.

After all is said and done and being a strong black woman, I am thankful that I was born a black African woman. I was brought up by extraordinarily strong women who taught and showed me that the world can be my oyster. I need to step up and enjoy it. I am encircled by love, unconditional love from friends turned sisters and family who accept, inspire, protect, love, correct, celebrate and appreciate me. With them I don't have to be anything but myself, whichever version of myself is present at that moment or day. On their wings, I soar...and not alone but with the entire flock.

Berenice Muller detailed the following:

Chapter 9 of the Constitution of South Africa promotes equality of all persons and the freedom from discrimination. The women's march of 1956 aimed at emancipating the women of South Africa, giving them a status that would undoubtedly be equal to that of a man. The status of women in South Africa still remains complicated. The objective of the march was to a certain extent achieved and there has been some improvement but there is still much that needs to be done to empower and improve the lives of women and girls. Every day we are struggling with unfair treatment in the workplace, sexual violence, domestic violence, gender inequality, oppression, discrimination, emotional abuse, navigating your career while maximising motherhood etc. The day-to day survival to many women is unnerving.

It is well documented that women are achieving new prominence in general with the 50% representation in leadership positions but the question is whether this reform is really yielding the results? The answer to this question is somehow subjective. The advocacy of 50% is taken seriously with the tone being set at the top from our political leaders for implementation downwards. Though the gender landscape changed drastically over the years with the inclusion of more women, many women still face challenges in achieving leadership positions because of the prejudice of men against women. Women are considered to be aligned with femininity and more often confronted with impediments such as motherhood, having too much family responsibilities, not being tough enough, lacking self-confidence, being emotional– that men do not have. These stereotypes, held by both men and often women, pose an important challenge to women in leadership and their effectiveness in their gender roles. If a woman takes on a leadership position must she contend with a man? For her to be accepted by both men and women must she be masculine, shave her hair, walk and talk like a man?

Though discrimination by men remains dominant in the workplace the worst discrimination is from another woman. How often do we hear from women 'I don't care who my boss is, as long as it's not a woman' or 'I get along better with a man than a woman, because women are emotional, moody and think they are superior? Or 'she thinks she is better than us because she is the manager'?

We as women are the first to criticise each other. We treat female leaders with less respect and support than male leaders. You expect to get better support from a woman because she understands your struggles better, but it becomes a rude awakening if the sisterhood is not there. It can be a case of jealousy, feeling threatened or because now that you are leading, your attitude towards other women has changed because of your success. There is so much for us as women to gain as a gender, in supporting each other instead of pulling each other down in an already male dominated environment where you are constantly feeling incompetent, oppressed and weak. We need an environment where we can safely discuss our challenges at work, or at home and simply acknowledge each other's success. In return, women leaders should not consider their status and success as a result of an individual struggle and support their female employees to become successful as well. We must present a united front and support each other's ideas and difficulties, otherwise men will continue to rule in the boardroom, make more money and look down on us.

Tshidi Mogorosi's views on GBV: *Every day I get reminded that my chances of dying a natural death are slim because I'm a woman. The killing of women and children is an uncontrollable pandemic in South Africa and we are losing this battle. Emotional, physical and financial abuse is rife in the society and we need to balance the scale. As much as we teach our girls to love themselves and be independent, we should give our boy child the same teaching about violence against women and children to reverse* *these ills in our society. We need to restore and rebuild our next generation regarding equity and humanity and, above all else, love.*

Mary-Vincent Dineo Ledwaba proposed self-love and awareness: *You are unique and beautifully created in the image of God. Remember it is important to always choose yourself and always put yourself first. When you know your worth, no one can make you worthless.*

Be strong, don't sit around feeling sorry for yourself, rise up and be in control. You are enough, forget about material things and focus on what lies in front of you. Surround yourself with positive people and seek respect not attention. Be you!

Conny Monoametsi felt it would be wrong for her not to say something: *We have heard the cries of women, some we don't see or know about, but we are affected one way or the other. It can be at work, home or socially. We need to stand together and fight the devil who gets between us, who undermines us and pulls us down. We can defeat him because nothing is impossible under the sun. Let us stand our ground and raise our voice to nail and expose the perpetrators. Together we can make this world a better place for us all.*

To you my husband, thank you for this wonderful book. I hope it reaches all men who want to make a difference in their lives and their women's lives. Let it be an eye opener to you and others. I pray that all the comments and contributions from the ladies sink into the minds of every man and woman who reads this book. It is our plea to men, to start treating us the way we deserve, like you as men would like to be treated. Allow us to be free, to exercise our freedom of speech and our freedom of movement, without fear. We are here to stay and we are not going anywhere. We are your mothers, wives, girlfriends, sisters and daughters. It is time to learn to live with us without treating us like slaves or possessions. Nurture us, water us, and allow us to be green inside and outside.

In Summary

Thank you to all the women who dedicated their time to send me their opinions and thoughts. I know it was a short notice. To those who couldn't send theirs, I understand and thank you too for your well wishes. To the women I didn't ask, please forgive me as there are only so many people I can ask, and that doesn't mean you are not important in my life. I have learnt a lot from all of you

I can never try to sum up what the women contribute and I understand that some things don't need interpretation. The Xhosa nation always says, "*IsiXhosa asitolikwa*" (Do not repeat an obvious thing, or, the nation is aware of).

9

CONCLUSION

I live with a motto that says, 'always reach for the sky, if you fail, come back with a little star to show that you have tried.' I have made too many mistakes in life and will still continue making mistakes since I'm human. That is the joy of being alive, make mistakes but learn and grow from them. "A mistake repeated more than once is a decision." Paulo Coelho.

Writing this book has been an eye opener for me. I have realised that people view things totally differently yet we learn from that if we are open minded. Nothing in life is guaranteed. We all have 24 hours in a day, how we each use it may be totally different and opportunity must always find you ready. You cannot dream of a car and not know how to drive or have a learner's or licence. Your dream will be valid, but it will take longer to fulfil because you won't be ready for the opportunity if it comes your way. You won't even see the opportunity.

Some people say opportunity is luck; I say luck is luck. If a stray bullet misses me by inches, I will definitely consider myself lucky or blessed, for that matter, but there might be an opportunity there waiting for me to tell my story. You are used to looking at negative things only instead of finding a niche market or being brave enough to step out of the comfort zone.

I believe there is so much potential in Africa and Africans, if we can unite and work together. We can build better education systems, build a better future for our children and totally take control of the economy by using our brains and skills.

As a man, I believe men must take the lead in the fight against gender-based violence. No one can resolve this if we as men don't take a stand. We are the major perpetrators. When women cry 'men stop killing us', they obviously don't mean all men. A sane man will know and understand that we need to do better. We need to teach and be present to the boy child; we need to instill direction. We need to learn to accept rejection. We need to learn to understand that these are our mothers, sisters, daughters, wives, girlfriends or extended girlfriends for that matter.

Some women have made bad choices, some lack direction on the way forward. This doesn't justify killing and abusing women. Because a lot of men have the same traits too. As men we must never fear the independence of women and their successes. If you are man and find yourself threatened by your woman, I suggest you talk to her about it and express your fears. If she loves you, she will be honest with you. If you cannot handle her, walk away in peace. Stay in your lane. Simple!

Lastly, we need to really learn how to manage money. Respect money. I say love it enough to ensure it stays with you. If you say it's evil, it will leave. Those who say money is evil, forget that every religion needs it. Why do they say the best things in life are free, yet truly we know everything has a price? As committed as you are to your family, friends, relationships, studies, work, sports teams and watching TV, you need the same effort to manage your money. Know where every cent goes. Let people call you thrifty, but you will be free. Living a debt free life is soothing to the soul. Poverty is the worst crime created by humans for other humans, and it must be eliminated.

In the end, we are trying this life thing, and it shows all of us flames, but we never give up. Try to read or learn a new craft, set goals, exercise and eat healthily whenever possible. Learn to prioritise things – not everything deserves your attention. If something is beyond your control, why sit and worry about it. Choose your battles. Choose your network and make it work for you. Don't just associate for the sake of association; build networks. You will come to realise that at times it's not about what you know but who you know. Introspect your attitude. Attitude can be good or bad, but it has no halfway. People who have the 'I don't care' attitude are only convincing themselves. Care a bit and look at yourself. Love yourself and appreciate yourself. No one will just come and help when you have a bad attitude.

Let's all be human and raise the spirit of UBUNTU.

Thank you. I leave you with these quotes:

> *"Success will never lower its standards to accommodate you. You have to raise your standards to achieve it. God provides food for every bird but not in its nest. Rise up to the challenges ahead of you and conquer your fears."*
>
> *"What counts in life is not the mere fact that we lived; it is what difference we have made to the lives of others that will determine the significance of the life we lead."*
> **—Nelson Mandela.**

10

DESCRIPTIONS/DEFINITIONS

- **Car making:** an art we created using old steel wardrobe hangers to make a car.

- **Chicago or Bathi:** agame played with stacked-up tins, where one player stands a few metres from the tins and throws a tennis ball at the tins to smash them. The opposing team will catch the ball and attempt to aim at the player who will be trying to repack the tins without being hit. The pain of the tennis ball hitting the player would deter anyone. Ladies were very active and extremely good at the game. They could throw the ball till you regretted playing.

- **Diketo:** is a coordination game where 10 small stones or marbles and one ghoen or big stone are made available for each player. A small hole of about 5cm deep is dug in the ground where the small stones will be placed for the player.

- **Draughts or checkers:** is a group of strategy board games for two players which involve diagonal moves of uniform game pieces and mandatory captures by jumping over opponent pieces. The name derives from the verb to draw or to move.

- **Feudalism:** the dominant social system in medieval Europe, in which the nobility held lands from the Crown in exchange for military service, and vassals were in turn tenants of the nobles, while the peasants (villains or serfs) were obliged to live on their lord's land and give him homage, labour, and a share of the produce, notionally in exchange for military protection.

- **Inculcation:** instil (an idea, attitude, or habit) by persistent instruction

- **Kite:** we actually made our own kites as kids but collected two straight sticks, placed them in a cross format and tied them with a thread. Then wrapped the one side of the stick in plastic.

- **Keti (sling):** we took a Y shaped stick, but it had to be proper, and tied it up with the old rubber bands from old tubes used in tyres. What you choose to use as a bullet for the sling determines the level of destruction. A stone, marble, or old mattress spring was called a V.

- **Morabaraba:** is a traditional two-player strategy board game played in South Africa and Botswana with a slightly different variation played in Lesotho. The game is known by many names in many languages, including *mlabalaba*, *mmela* (in Setswana), muravava, and *umlabalaba*.

- **Scotch**: played by drawing blocks in the sand or stoop and a round flat tin filled with sand. That tin would be thrown into the block and a player would attempt to kick the tin into all boxes drawn. Players would take turns and whoever completed first would be the winner.

- **Stena (with marbles):** the game is played by placing two bricks together on the long side, with two finger spaces between them. Players took turns to shoot a marble into the small space. The player who succeeds first, wins. This is what could be defined as township golf.

- **Tiki-Line:** the term was made famous by old people, particularly women, who would use it as a derogatory word against other women who lacked moral values. Apparently, those women used to go around asking men for money (tiki was the olden day coin money). The women would do anything for that tiki, as I was told.

- **Umgusha or kgati or skipping**: the game was played with old unwanted pantyhose, torn into long pieces and joined so that two people could hold either end, while a third person jumped over it. The luxury of having skipping rope was nonexistent.

- **Ludo**: is derived from Latin, meaning 'I play'. It is a strategy board game for two to four players, in which the players race their four *tokens* from start to finish according to the roll of dice.

11

REFERENCES

A brief history of education: https://www.psychologytoday.com/za/blog/freedom-learn/200808/brief-history-education (Accessed June 2020)

An examination of causes of educational inequity: https://edsurgeindependent.com/the-current-education-system-is-failing-our-students-b35614943541 (Accessed June 2020)

Stokvels: https://www.iol.co.za/business-report/economy/sa-stok-vels-collectively-save-r44bn-annually-25814087 (Accessed June 2020)

Rudzani Mulaudzi on stokvels: https://www.gsb.uct.ac.za/stokvels (Accessed June 2020)

Taxi Industry: https://www.businessinsider.co.za/how-big-is-south-african-taxi-industry-2019-5 (Accessed June 2020)

10 SA Entrepreneurs who built their businesses from nothing: https://www.entrepreneur.com/article/327431 (Accessed June 2020)

Stats SA: https://www.timeslive.co.za/news/south-africa/2019-11-18-whites-earn-three-times-more-than-black-people-stats-sa/ (Accessed June 2020)

Everything you need to know about SA's government workers: https://businesstech.co.za/news/government/113488/everything-you-need-to-know-about-sas-government-workers (Accessed June 2020)

https://www.gems.gov.za/en/corporate/about-gems/fact-sheet (Accessed June 2020)

Personal finance: https://www.investopedia.com/terms/p/personalfinance.asp (Accessed June 2020)

Investment Scams: Sue Torr: https://www.moneyweb.co.za/financial-advisor-views/how-to-spot-an-investment-scam/ (Accessed June 2020)

GBV: https://www.saferspaces.org.za/understand/entry/gender-based-violence-in-south-africa (Accessed June 2020)

12

ADDITIONAL READING
MATERIAL

Moroka Modiba, 2007. *Think Yourself Rich*: A step-by-step guide to financial independence. 1st ed. Penguin Random House, South Africa.

Phumelele Ndumo, 2011. *From Debt to Riches*: Steps to financial success. 13th impression. Jacana.

Gerald Mwandiambira, 2016. *Money*: A financial planning guide for ordinary people. 2nd ed. Tracey MacDonald Publishers.

Dr Joseph Murphy, 2018. *The Power of Your Subconscious Mind*: 1st ed. Simon & Schuster UK Ltd.

Robin Sharma, 2010. *The Leader Who Had no Title*: A modern fable on real success in business and in life. 1st ed. Simon & Schuster UK Ltd

13

RECOGNITION OF CONTRIBUTIONS

- Sue Torr, Managing Director at Crue Invest (Pty) Ltd, for an article on how to spot an investment scam.

- Dr Peter Grey, on an extract about the history of education.

- Will Kenton, on a personal finance article under basic household/ personal financial management for financial freedom.

ABOUT THE AUTHOR

Tebogo Kenneth Monoametsi was born in Soweto, Meadowlands Zone 1. He is currently working for the Department of COGHSTA in the Northern Cape Province. Tebogo is a well-equipped Public Supply Chain Manager, highly focused management professional with over 19 years' working experience within both private-sector and public-sector environments. He has a BComm in Accounting and Auditing, BComm in Risk Management and a Master's in Business Leadership with an elective major in Supply Chain Management. He is a member of the Chartered Institute of Procurement and Supply (CIPS).

He obtained his Master's thesis with a distinction and won an award for his ground-breaking research on: "A conceptual framework for the successful implementation of green supply chain management practices in the public sector."

Tebogo is a pioneering individual who welcomes challenges and strives to achieve best practices by identification, creation and implementation of solutions through accurate analysis and information collaboration. A team player, leader and motivator.

Contact Details:
Email address: tkmonoametsi@conteb.co.za
Website: www.conteb.co.za

REVIEWS

Yes, I'm Generalising, a book which touches every aspect of trauma and emphasises the battles which everyone, men and women, encounter throughout life.

I loved reading the book as it opened my eyes to many issues I was not aware of because I had my own wallowing taking place inside. The book gives insight on how to work with finances, effects of debt, violence against both women and men, and creates an overall atmosphere of understanding not only your own battles but also those of others.

I strongly believe the advice of this book will bring about a positive impact to all, but especially to the woman who has withdrawn from society and is hiding in a pit due to the trauma experienced in her life. Thus, this book will assist her to rise from that rut she is in and rise above to whatever heights she can achieve. In addition, it will change the mindset of men who still hold onto the traditional teachings that a woman is only good enough for doing chores around the home, looking after kids, cooking, cleaning, etc.

Yes, I'm Generalising inspires, uplifts the soul and brings about a sense of faith that there can be a better tomorrow.

—Chrisie Adams

The topics covered in this book, can be books on their own, hence my view that it's many books in one. But the way the author approaches the topics draws you in to read more. I'm not someone who reads books generally (trust me a habit rather difficult to kick), but I found myself reading through the book. Topics like the schooling system in our country, financial health, work relations in the private and public sector and gender-based violence, is a wide spread and you get the author's views on them. He's no expert on some of these things, but this is not an expert writing a book, just observations of a layman from his own life experience.

The section on gender-based violence (I thought the entire book is about that initially) stands out to me given the times we are living in, in South Africa.

It includes violence against the LGBTI community in the country. And in as much as he does highlight that men do experience violence from women, the author emphasises that women suffer the most abuse and violence at the hands of men. This fact is often used to muddy the waters whenever this topic comes up, but I'm glad this author doesn't fall into that trap and stays on point with our issues generally with violence against women and children.

The book challenged me to have a view or challenged the views I had about some of the topics covered. This is the author's take on these topics, we all have opinions on some of the topics, the author was just brave enough to put them on paper.

—Felex Nkambule

I really enjoyed reading the book. The intro was a bit short. I wish you went a bit deeper into your upbringing to give other readers a glimpse of how it all influenced your thinking and observations about life.

I am happy you covered highly important topics of our daily lives and struggles:

- The outdated education system
- The emancipation of a black mind
- Basic household/personal financial management for financial freedom.
- GBV – violence against our grandmothers, mothers, sisters, daughters, wives and children. Thank you on this one. As you would say there's something wrong with us men. Factory fault...
- Voices of the powerless but powerful – *imbokoto* – sad to hear the fears of the ones we are meant to protect and love.

This book will change people's lives, give them hope, financial management skills, and emancipate their minds. Well done and congratulations on your book.

—Jeff Pitsoe

Well Done Mjita, it's a great book that is needed in our society. Great initiative.

—Siphiwe Fakude